Empower Yourself with Knowledge.

Did You Know . . .

- "Old-fashioned" talk therapies are the first and best way to treat children's problems. (See page 8)
- Learning disorders tend to run in families. Discover how to tell if your child is at risk. (See page 116)
- Bed-wetting is most common in shy or anxious children. But it *can* be overcome. (See page 151)
- Not all forms of stress are bad or abnormal: Some stress is essential to a child's ability to function and be productive. (See page 10)
- Teenagers who had ADD as children are more likely to abuse drugs and suffer from poor self-esteem. Find out how to spot the early warning signs. (See page 108)
- The more a parent interacts and bonds with a child—starting in infancy—the more fully developed his or her intelligence will be. (See page 121)
- Childhood depression is most often caused by environmental stresses. Among them: parental fighting, domestic violence, lack of constructive reinforcement, and neglect. (See page 5)

D0150223

Is My Child OK?

When Behavior Is a Problem, When It's Not, and When to Seek Help

Henry A. Paul, M.D.

A DELL TRADE PAPERBACK

A DELL TRADE PAPERBACK

Published by
Dell Publishing
a division of
Random House, Inc.
1540 Broadway
New York, New York 10036

Book design by Maura Fadden Rosenthal

Dell books may be purchased for business or promotional use or for special sales. For information please write to: Special Markets Department, Random House, Inc., 1540 Broadway, New York, NY 10036.

DTP and the colophon are trademarks of Random House, Inc.

Library of Congress Cataloging-in-Publication Data
Paul, Henry A.
　　Is my child ok? : when behavior is a problem, when it's not, and when to seek help / Henry A. Paul.
　　　　p.　　cm.
　　ISBN 0-440-50887-8
　　1. Problem children—Counseling of.　2. Problem children—Family relationships.　3. Child rearing.　4. Parent and child.　5. Child psychology. 6. Behavior disorders in children.　I. Title.
HQ733+　P38　2000
649'.153—dc21

00-025332

Printed in the United States of America

Published simultaneously in Canada

September 2000

10　9　8　7　6　5　4　3　2　1
FFG

This book is dedicated to my wife, Carol,
whose loving parenting of our children continues
to be a source of hope, growth, and wonderment.

ACKNOWLEDGMENTS

I wish to acknowledge Guy Kettelhack for his constructive criticism, sense of humor, humility, enormous knowledge, and unending support.

CONTENTS

SECTION THREE
LEARNING AND SCHOOL

SECTION FOUR
THE BODY

SECTION FIVE
SEXUALITY

SECTION SIX
FAMILY

SECTION SEVEN
GLOBAL DISORDERS

SECTION EIGHT
GETTING HELP

INTRODUCTION

Anxious Questions and Optimistic Answers: Assessing What's Emotionally "Normal" for Your Child

In more than twenty-five years of seeing thousands of parents and children in my clinical practice as a psychiatrist, four words—expressed in the form of one anxious question—have probably been repeated in my office more often than any others: "Is my child normal?" Sometimes the question is spoken; sometimes—maybe more often—I read it in a parent's eyes.

The anxiety felt by parents who ask me this question is usually quite different from the anxiety they may feel in a medical doctor's office when a child is physically ill. Physical illness is commonly perceived as something "objective" that appropriate medical treatment can cure. But when a child is depressed, agitated, withdrawn, or aggressive, or otherwise gives expression to emotional distress and confusion that seem to have no clear cause, parents often feel they are on far less sure ground. Children—especially *our* children—aren't supposed to have "emotional problems." We want to believe childhood will be our sons' and daughters' one period of relatively uncomplicated happiness and innocence. But often by the time parents contact me, their children have already had a rocky time, and any hope of an untroubled childhood has already faded. The problem may manifest itself in poor grades in school, a child's inability to get along well with other children, or private habits or behavior that parents find alien, bewildering, and, well, "abnormal." The whole family may be distressed because a child is not reacting in some expected or hoped-for way.

Happily, in the great majority of cases, the answer to "Is my child normal?" is yes. Many if not most parental anxieties about the normality of a child's emotional distress or development turn out to be groundless: There's a great deal of latitude in what's "normal" for children at virtually every developmental stage. But the acuteness and persistence of this parental anxiety is worrying because of the self-doubt from which it often stems. Too often it signals mothers' and fathers' strong mistrust of their own parenting perceptions, aptitudes, and abilities. Cowed by the presumed expertise of a therapist or other mental health-care professional, frightened by news reports of psychotic kids gunning other children down in schools (which imply that children may be more dangerously unpredictable and less manageable than any unaided mother or father is equipped to deal with), too many parents feel they must favor the "official" assessment (though sometimes based on only an hours-long relationship with the child) over their own ideas and speculations (based, of course, on a lifelong relationship with the child).

It's not that the professional's expertise isn't important or, indeed, often essential—many crucial diagnoses and treatments cannot be determined without it. But that so many parents undervalue their own expertise keeps them from contributing as much as they could to their child's welfare, both directly at home and informationally to the expert whose help the child may need. Parents know far more than they're aware they know. They can offer a professional diagnostician essential data about the child's past and present that usually cannot be determined in any other way. Parents can do this not only because they have more information about their children than anyone else, but because they have such a profound, loving investment in their children's growth and happiness. This love is what enables a parent to help heal a child—usually more effectively than any outside "expert" could hope to do.

What Is an Emotionally Healthy Child?

What do we want for our children? What is the definition of emotional health we would apply to them? What might we posit for our children as emotional goals?

Good emotional health has a number of components of which most parents I know seem to be cognizant, and indeed generally quite consciously wish for their children. Articulating them is helpful because it reminds us how full and balanced a range of feelings, abilities, and capacities good emotional health requires.

Certainly we want our children to have a firm enough sense of identity not to be swayed too easily by external pressures. On the other hand, we want our children to be able to interact with others receptively and with respect for others' differing opinions; we do not want them to be locked into so fixed an identity that they become inflexible and intolerant. In other words, emotionally healthy children will know their own positions but also be able to go along with others without a sense of defeat or loss of self. This ability to live with and among others while also maintaining a sense of self depends on two correlative abilities: to tolerate difference and to detect commonality. Such a child will have the peace of mind to be able freely and securely to know and express him- or herself and also be able to interact with others and learn from them. This child will be able to oppose and comply, be with others and be with him- or herself, move ahead and wait patiently, compete with and get along with others. An emotionally healthy child grows with self-respect as s/he learns to respect others. S/he will grow to appreciate his or her uniqueness and that of others while also appreciating similarities. S/he will know his or her own values and respect those of others.

How do we help our children to achieve this balanced emotional health?

The main task is to create an environment conducive to it.

While inevitably there are genetic components in a child's emotional makeup, susceptibilities, and temperament, environment plays as crucial a role—perhaps more crucial simply because it is the only half of the equation we can affect (we can't change anybody's genes yet). The child's prospects for good emotional health are highest when his or her world is constructive, fair, warm, interested in his or her growth, encouraging, loving, and genuinely appreciative of his or her uniqueness. This, of course, describes an ideal; creating such an environment involves a host of difficulties that probably can never be entirely surmounted. As parents, we always bring to the mix our own emotional baggage, blind spots, unconscious strivings and wishes, unfulfilled personal needs, and vicarious expectations (felt by our children as demands and pressures)—attitudes based more on competition or blind adherence to the status quo than on a more objective appreciation of our child's unique assets and desires. We can make strides to combat and lessen if not eradicate some of these impediments, but none of us is perfect; often we can only hope to create an environment that is, *on balance,* nutritive.

No One Knows Your Child Better than You

In addition to creating—or at least grappling to create—a healthier environment for our children, are there measures we can employ to make sure our children develop their unique capacities (which at the same time means developing the healthiest possible sense of self)? To get clear about how we may be able to help our children, we first have to make sure that we are seeing them as clearly as we can. To reiterate: *No one knows your child better than you.* This does not mean that you can't (or shouldn't) get to know your child better— indeed, I'll be offering a questionnaire later on that will help you to do just that. But I italicize it to emphasize how important it is to realize and acknowledge what you do know about your child, especially what you may have either blocked out as unimportant or simply not looked at as the helpful data it can be. Most parents have been with their children since conception and birth—and certainly from a very tender age. They have fed, diapered, disciplined, shared joy and frustration with, soothed, held, been awakened by and slept with, worried about, nursed back to health, and closely observed almost all of their children's developmental progressions. Who knows their children's biological rhythms better? Their likes and dislikes? Their abilities, preferences, talents, and shortcomings? No one makes a better diagnostician than an attentive parent.

You see in your answers to the foregoing questions just some of the rich evidence for my claim that parents often are their children's best diagnosticians. Of course, sometimes conditions and afflictions your child may face will require a response from a trained professional, not just a loving, supportive parent. Various types of educational and clinical training are required to make formal diagnoses and to employ certain therapeutic interventions. However, parents can help with the great bulk of emotional challenges that children face—help that becomes more effective the more consciously parents acknowledge what they know about their children (so that they can gain a clearer picture of who their children really are), as well as create the most nurturing environment possible for their children's growth.

Beyond Pathology:
Seeing Symptoms as Communication

No human being's progress through childhood is exactly the same as any other's. While we can attach the achievement of certain developmental milestones to certain very general ages, each of us navigates them (learning how to walk, speak, control our bowels and bladder, bond with and separate from parents or caretakers, interact socially, etc.) in quite unique ways and according to differing timetables. The constant and continually changing confluence of nature and nurture—a child's genetic inheritance and the effects on the child of the environment (parental care and expectations, cultural pressures, and the like)—provide a kaleidoscope of influence and reaction that makes each of our journeys through childhood even less predictable. *Not* to experience conflict and stress throughout this maelstrom of internal and external influences would be abnormal; some degree of friction and anxiety is inevitable. When a child hits a snag—when for a moment s/he halts, regresses, or becomes confused at one or another developmental crossroads—and the snag manifests as what the literature calls a "disturbance" (some perceived abnormality in feeling, behavior, or thinking), worried parents often scurry to doctors and psychiatrists and bookstores and TV talk shows for guidance. In fact, the disturbance almost always represents a completely ordinary glitch in the particular child's path. The best advice to such parents is to relax and wait for the symptom they're worried about to pass on its own—because it most likely will.

Indeed, as you'll see in our discussion of many symptoms and conditions covered in this book, children often experience more pain and difficulty from their parents' reactions to whatever disturbances they may exhibit than from the disturbances themselves. Be reassured, first of all, that nearly all children manifest symptoms—some of them quite weird and frightening—as a normal response to the struggle of becoming themselves; rarely is it evidence of sickness requiring professional intervention. This is not to say that you don't need to attend to them. These symptoms are your child's way of communicating his or her distress, as well as a flag for you to see what assistance you might be able to provide to help the child through a rocky period. They are for the most part transient reminders that life is not perfect for any of us and that under stress the human psyche resorts to an ingenious array of tactics to vent that distress and ease pressure felt to be intolerable.

The Bigger Picture: Sorting Out Your Child's Temperament from Your Own

The individual ways children grow and express themselves constitute what might be thought of as each child's particular style of reaction or response. There may be no more important child-rearing enterprise for you as a parent than to be able to identify and learn as much as possible about your children's styles or patterns of response so that you can begin to determine what emotional reactions are normal for each child. Too often parents tend to see as pathology what are in their children really perfectly normal traits; this is particularly the case when such traits differ from the parents' own.

The following two sets of questions are designed to help you to identify the influences and effects that make your children and you the unique individuals you are. The first set of questions addresses your child's temperament and personality, and should help you gain a more objective picture of your child. Many of the pressures we place on our children stem from assumptions and expectations that may apply to us but do not apply to them. We go a long distance toward easing that pressure and helping our children to fulfill their unique potential by stepping back to sort out who they are and how they may be different from us. The second set of questions will help you to assess your own temperament as a parent and the influences in your home life. So many conflicts in family life and between parents and children proceed from not acknowledging our different personalities and assumptions. To make this acknowledgment, not only do we have to understand who our children are as individuals, but we also need to become aware of our own styles of response so that we can identify assumptions that may have caused us to impose unfair expectations on our children, whose temperaments, needs, dreams, and desires may be quite different from our own.

Remember that the aim in answering the following questions is not to make any diagnosis or decision or take any particular actions. These questions are simply designed to help you acquire information about your child and yourself—to help you get to know and acknowledge some of the character traits and propensities that are natural to each of you, and to take note of some of the influences in your home life with which you both have to deal.

Your Child's Temperament and Personality

1. What are your child's strengths, talents, strong points, proclivities, and most creative characteristics? Are you encouraging these assets and talents even though they may differ from your own?

2. How would you describe your child's mode of interacting with others? Appeasing, attempting to please? Dependent? Shy? Good-natured? Sharing? Submissive? Aggressive? Dominating? Intrusive? Demanding? Defiant? Oppositional? Spacy? Dreamy? Independent? Distant? Most children show one predominant set of characteristics at any particular phase of childhood (they may be different at another stage), although others are also present. Do you respect your child's mode of relating to others, or do you try to bend that mode so the child will "fit in"?

3. Does your child remind you of anyone else in the family? What do you think of whoever that person is? Has this made you quietly worried? Has the perceived similarity prejudiced you toward the child?

4. Is your child naturally sedentary or active? You can often see this from birth on. Is he or she restless, spon-

taneous, vigorous, "all over the place," wiggly, and fidgety? Or does s/he just sit there, tend to be immobile, seem to move in slow motion?

5. Children have a variety of moods, but characteristically they have a predominant proclivity for one mood. What is that predominant mood for your child? Happy? Irritable? Sad? Pensive? Pleasant? Positive? Negative? Frowner? Smiler? Angry? Hard to please? Whiner? Anxious?

6. Is your child flexible or rigid in adapting to new circumstances? Is s/he slow or fast to make contact with others? Is s/he shy or reticent? Does s/he have to have it all his or her way? Does s/he throw a tantrum or go with the flow when things don't go his or her way? What are your child's usual reactions to new people, routines, foods, and so on?

7. Is your child regular in his or her habits (eating, sleeping, eliminating, social and school routines), or does life for your child seem to be a haphazard series of irregular, unscheduled, and disorganized events?

8. Is your child mild and placid, or do you expect intense and even explosive reactions to many different situations? Is every feeling a deep one, expending a lot of energy, or is your child much less reactive, even disquietingly cool?

9. Does your child pay attention, follow through, and persist in a task until it is completed, or is s/he distracted by any stimulus that happens to come his or her way? Are things left undone? Does his or her attention seem to wander? Does s/he daydream?

10. On the whole, does your child seem sensitive or insensitive to such environmental stimuli as smells, noise, tastes, textures, and colors? Does s/he readily respond to or tend to ignore social cues?

11. Is your child easily frustrated, or does s/he seem to have a high threshold before becoming disturbed or upset?

Assessing Your Temperament and the Influences in Your Home Life

1. Review the foregoing questions about your child and now answer them for yourself. Note what you perceive to be the similarities and differences between you and your child.

2. What kind of person are you? Do you see yourself as similar to or different from your child? Do you perceive a "good fit" between you and your child, or do you feel you have to go out of your usual way to cater to his or her needs? Do you feel willing to go out of your way to accommodate the child, or do you feel the child should adjust to those around him or her?

3. How were you raised? What was your place in the sibling order? Was it same as your child? What are your feelings about that? How were emotions, differences, compromise, sharing, and needs for distance or closeness handled in your home? How was anger handled by your parents?

4. Were there any serious mental problems in any family members? How did this affect you? Did it scare you, or were you able to empathize? Do you worry about your child being sick? Do you overidentify your child with any particular relative?

5. Have there been upheavals, changes, losses, or deaths in your family? How have they affected you and other members of your family?

6. What kind of family tone is present in your home? Is it loud, expressive, emotional? Is it quiet, restrained, get-down-to-business? Are feelings shared and respected, or are they minimized or rationalized away?

Is there room for error in your home, or are serious standards of performance and conduct upheld? Is the atmosphere severe and intimidating or loose and free? Is there a lot of concern about what the neighbors think? Is the family close? Is there much contact with the extended family, or does the nuclear family tend to shut itself away from the outside?

How to Use This Book

This book is organized by, and designed to be consulted according to, symptoms—that is, by looking through the table of contents, you should easily be able to find the chapter or chapters that apply to the questions or concerns you have about your child at that moment.

These symptoms are broken down into eight broad categories:

- FEELINGS (symptoms and disorders that express themselves most directly through emotions, such as depression, grief, anger, anxiety, etc.)
- BEHAVIOR ("acting-out" problems ranging from bullying and fighting to fire setting)
- LEARNING AND SCHOOL (learning disorders, underachievement, intelligence, school phobia, etc.)
- THE BODY (somatic problems ranging from bed-wetting to tics)
- SEXUALITY (sexual development, masturbation, gender identity, etc.)
- THE FAMILY (from adoption and single-parent families to the varying impacts on a child of depressed, alcoholic, or physically ill parents)
- GLOBAL DISORDERS (such severe but rare disorders as schizophrenia and autism)
- GETTING HELP (a discussion of therapies, medications, and testing)

Each entry includes a general discussion of the topic indicating, where appropriate, the "normal" parameters of what is often a transient condition or behavior that need not overly concern you, as well as signs of more serious trouble, when professional attention or intervention may be indicated. This is followed by a "What to Do" section that offers suggestions you can generally follow yourself with your child at home, as well as a rundown of what professional help or intervention may be advisable in the event that the problem is more serious.

As you'll see, many of the individual entries within each of these categories overlap to some degree with entries in other categories. In particular, the effects of the family are almost always pervasive and in some way implicated in almost every difficulty the child faces. With this in mind, at the end of nearly every chapter within these categories you'll see a "See Also" section with a list of related chapters. Scan the information in the chapters listed, even if their chapter titles may appear to have little to do with why you picked up the book at that moment. You may well find something illuminating in the cross-referenced chapter: a deeper or enriched definition, a wider perspective, or a view of treatment options you may not have considered. Also, there is a resource section listing national organizations involved with both mental health in general and specific disorders or problems.

FEELINGS

CHAPTER ONE

Depression and Mania

"At first Joey just seemed sad about Lucky, our dog, having to be put to sleep. But he never snapped out of it. He's always in his room, won't talk, go to school, or even eat much. He's lost weight and stays up real late. And now he's saying he wants to go to heaven with Lucky."

We all have moods and feeling states. Some days we're up and some days we're down. Some days we're irritable, angry, and on edge, while other days everything is coming up roses. Children have moods just as adults do, and with children we can often see frequent mood changes—sometimes even many times in one day. Just think of children who cry with frustration only to be exuberant upon getting a favored toy just an hour or two later. How many times have we seen an increasingly excited, even giggly child quickly deteriorate into tears when others don't appreciate his fooling around? The thing to remember is that moods are normal. They're as valuable as the colors of a picture. They add depth to our everyday experience. Without feelings and moods our children would simply be robotlike, carrying out developmental tasks in a lifeless fashion. Essentially, children without feeling states would have no identity. We are what we feel.

Every child is born with the capacity to have a wide array of feelings. But each child also has a particular tone, an individual range, and specific ways of expressing these feelings. This results from a combination of innate temperamental differences as well as the influences of the family feeling states to which he is exposed. Parents should become familiar with their children's feeling states: what brings them on, how long they last, whether they are flexible, and whether they overwhelm the child too often.

One of the most common feeling states that children have is sadness. A child can experience this mood from a host of situations, such as disappointment, loss of a family member or pet, frustration in a social setting, unanswered needs, moving to a new neighborhood and losing old friends—the list goes on and on. Sometimes this sad mood can come from a dream a child may not even remember he had. He'll just awaken sad. Normal sadness is usually self-limited and doesn't seriously interfere with the everyday life of a child. There might be some tears, some withdrawal, even a tendency to be irritable, sullen, pouty, or whiny. But it usually passes with a sympathetic attitude by parents. Even leaving the child alone to work things out on his own might be all that's necessary to create a situation where a child returns to his usual everyday feeling state. Sadness is a part of life. Parents should not interfere with this. Only when sadness becomes depression should they be concerned.

Sadness doesn't turn into depression until certain mood features enter the picture. A depressed child is different from a sad one. Depressive feelings usually seem deeper than regular sadness. There is often a lot of anger and irritability involved as well. Additionally, sleep is often disturbed, appetite is diminished, and the child may lose weight. Depressed children often have problems in school because they are preoccupied and can't focus well. They are often tired from not sleeping, as well as fatigued due to the depression itself. Most important, depressed children often feel some combination of feeling they are bad, guilty, of low self-esteem, and even worthless. They often feel hopeless as well. Telltale signs of depression often appear in body language: a sad face, a tired look, slumped shoulders, a head held down, apprehensiveness, and a generalized appearance of apathy. School-age children who are depressed will tell you that other kids are better than they are, that no one likes them, and that they are inferior in some way or another. Often they get physical signs and symptoms such as headaches, stomachaches, nausea, or muscular pains. Children who are depressed often think about dying. Some contemplate suicide, and some even try.

Depression runs the gamut from low level to high level. Sometimes it's mixed with a lot of irritability, and sometimes it just looks like plain old tired despair—life in painful slow motion.

Depression can affect children of all ages, but it is more likely to occur in older children. In the school years it generally appears as described in the previous paragraphs. In the preschool years it often presents as a feeding difficulty, clinginess, poor development, sleeping problems, intestinal distress, and sometimes difficulty attaching to important people in the environment.

Depression is mostly caused by stress in the environment. Of course, there has to be a genetic predisposition to handling stress in this way, and it is interesting that most stressed children don't develop depression and most children with an inherited tendency to depression don't get depressed either.

What are the stresses that commonly cause depression? Parental fighting, domestic violence, child abuse or neglect, anxiety and anger in the child that go unheeded by parents, lack of constructive reinforcement, and sometimes learning to be helpless and ineffectual by modeling oneself on those in the environment.

It wasn't long ago that mania was considered nonexistent in children. It has always been known in adults, where it presents as a feeling state characterized by elation, euphoria, ebullience, and even ecstasy combined with grandiosity, racing thoughts, rapid speech, distractibility, hyperactivity, and decreased need for sleep, as well as dangerous impulsive activities such as sexual promiscuity and financial indiscretion. This abnormal mood often alternates with depression in the same individual, thus the term manic-depression (now called bipolar illness). Until lately there was not much research on bipolar illness in younger people. We now know that some children considered hyperactive and even some psychotic children have been misdiagnosed. These children are actually presenting with mania in childhood. They often look like children with attention deficit disorder or another behavioral disorder because they can be hyperactive, seem irritable, talk rapidly, and are distractible and emotionally difficult to handle. A professional will differentiate them from children with attention deficit disorder in that the latter show the symptoms of attention deficit disorder earlier in life and rarely exhibit the abnormally high moods, the heightened feelings of "happiness," and often the irritability seen in children who are manic. Manic children are extremely difficult to handle and often need to be hospitalized because of their impulsivity and their disruption of the environment. Recent research has shown that some people destined to develop bipolar illness often present with mania early in life. The diagnosis of mania is a difficult one to make and is often made after treatment for a behavior disorder or attention deficit disorder has failed.

WHAT TO DO

If your child has one or more signs of depression for a few weeks and seems not to be improving, you should intervene in the following way:

1. Speak to your child in a gentle way; criticism, even constructive criticism, is often misperceived by a depressed child and is further reason to dislike him- or herself.

2. Use common sense and ask if there is a particular thought or situation that is bothering him or her.

3. Help a child locate possible triggers by going over a time line of possibilities: when you noticed signs of

depression, what s/he might have been doing or expressing or experiencing in school, with friends, at camp, or even at home. Trying to link up feelings and particular stressful situations is very helpful. Remember also that the trigger might be you or your family situation, and that is a more difficult one to face and certainly to examine and change.

4. Be hopeful, but not falsely so. Reassure your child that there is probably a good reason—that is, an understandable reason—for him or her to be depressed.

5. If you locate the trigger, let the child express his or her despair even if it seems unreasonable or irrational. That expression and your reception can be curative in itself since it heightens the child's sense of attachment and lessens his or her feeling of alienation. After this expression you might tell your child how common it is to have such feelings but that there might be other ways to respond to a situation.

6. You might want to share similar experiences you had, not necessarily telling your child intimate details of your life, but enough simply to add a measure to his or her optimism and hopefulness.

7. Try to keep in mind that most depressions are self-limiting and most children get better within several weeks to a couple of months on their own.

8. The following signs indicate that professional help is needed:

   • Thoughts or allusions to dying, death, heaven, afterlife, dead relatives or pets; severe guilt and/or feelings of "badness"; the wish to "not be here"; suicidal statements, thoughts, gestures, or actions

   • Depression that does not respond to the above measures over a period of several weeks

   • Worsened depression over several weeks

- Low-grade depression that continues for several months
- Severe disruption in school attendance, social interactions, or physical health

Keep in mind that children with certain conditions are more prone to depression than others. This includes children of depressed parents, those with a behavior disorder or attention deficit disorder, those with a problem in development, and certainly children who have severe social difficulties due to shyness and fear.

9. There are many treatments for depression but none as important as psychotherapy—individual, family, and sometimes even group therapy. These "old-fashioned" talk therapies should always be the first and main treatment, since understanding and communicating with someone about feelings still affords the most relief. Of course, in cases of suicidal emergency, severe school and social failure, or severe physical symptoms, sometimes a child may have to be hospitalized, but this is quite uncommon. The use of antidepressant medication has been dramatically increasing over the years. We are beginning to see some studies of the use of antidepressants (approved for adults) in children. Antidepressants have saved many lives from the ravages of depression. It is safe to say that their use in children, despite being less than fully informed, can be quite helpful, but unless severity dictates their use it is safe to say that the first tool in treatment should remain psychotherapy and not drugs.

10. Mania in children, as mentioned above, is often diagnosed after other diagnoses and medications have been tried. This symptom often responds well to mood-stabilizing and/or antipsychotic medications in addition to psychotherapy.

SEE ALSO

Learning Disorders

The Underachiever

All Types of Therapy

Psychotropic Medication
  and Children

Attachment Disorders

Attention Deficit Disorder

Behavior Disorders

Shyness

Child Physical Abuse

Anxiety

Anger

CHAPTER TWO
Stress

"Right after the break-in we were all a little stressed and scared. But Janey still can't sleep, worries all the time, jumps if she hears a noise, and says that sometimes she even thinks she sees the burglar in the hall entering our room, just like he did."

Stress—internal or environmental pressure that we register as coercive or threatening—has become a hot topic for a simple reason: None of us escapes it. Daily we undergo an unprecedented barrage of warring stimuli from the media. Assumptions once held to be normal or foregone about identity, family, success, and sexuality have all broken down, and we often feel as if we have to "invent" ourselves and our lives with very little dependable help or guidance. Life is arguably more stressful now than at any other time in history—never have we had to balance such an onslaught of different influences, options, and obligations. It's no wonder that so much attention is now being paid to it.

All stress is not bad or abnormal; a certain amount of stress is essential to functioning well. We couldn't accomplish anything without it. Meeting deadlines at work, responding to basic responsibilities in the family, finishing what we start, and making long-term plans to achieve larger goals all depend upon reacting in positive ways to normal, productive, and manageable stress. But where do we draw the line between this useful stress and the excessive, overly coercive, damaging stress that can push us over the edge into physical and psychic illness? This question is particularly difficult to answer for children. Child development might be seen, in fact, as the successful sequential adaptation to new and necessary stages of stress—learning how to walk, eat, talk, use the bathroom, interact socially, ride a bike, spell, add and subtract, delay gratification. These all involve dealing with inevitable frustrations—stresses—that we must overcome in order to mature.

But the overall stress outlook for children is just as worrying as it is for adults. In addition to the normal stressful adaptations of growing up, many children have to deal with such traumas as moving from neighborhood to neighborhood, divorced parents, changing schools, or physical illness. Many children deal with increased expectations from their parents for social and academic achievement, learning sometimes as early as nursery school to be competitive with other children—to "win" at all costs. Note the increasing numbers of "stage parents" and "coaches." Images of violence abounding in the media, from hurricanes, tornadoes, and earthquakes to mass murders and rapes, add more stress. Sexual excess is unavoidable, as afternoon TV talk shows and Internet chat rooms afford children an unwelcome riot of disturbing, confusing, and undeniably stressful influences.

It's important to remember that, as with every other influence, different children respond differently to stress—and not always with the same degree of harm or negative outcome. Some children seem temperamentally able to roll with the punches better than others. What one child finds overly stressful, another child may simply see as a challenge. This is one more reason why it is essential for parents continually to assess their children's temperaments and styles of expression and response: You need to see, and to some degree treat, each child as the unique human being s/he is, particularly with regard to increasing or decreasing the stresses in that child's life. Pushing one child to try harder, allowing another child more latitude—these are decisions that depend upon your sensitive understanding of the personality of each individual child and the nature of the stresses s/he happens to be facing.

Some stresses, however, are traumatic for any child. A traumatic stressor can be defined as something occurring outside the usual events of childhood that threatens a child's life or physical integrity and which the child experiences firsthand (sexual abuse, severe illness, car crash, etc.) or must confront in someone else's life (a family member's illness or sudden death, etc.). Fortunately, when most children register something as a harmful or traumatic stressor, while they will tend to remember it with some vividness, they are able to keep themselves together. They may wonder why it happened and go through a period of what is called omen formation in which they try to reason out "Why me?" Right after a trauma, children usually experience short-lived disturbances in sleep, difficulties with schoolwork, or an inability to sustain focus or attention on a particular task, and they often develop either fears that the trauma will recur or more general fears of being alone (for example, being separated from their parents), making them vulnerable to the recurrence of trauma. They may dream of it or have seemingly unrelated but terrifying nightmares caused by the anxiety of dealing with the ordeal. Nearly every child will play games and draw pictures that in some way depict or reflect the trauma—in fact, as with sexual abuse, the games the child enacts with stuffed animals or dolls may be the only expression the child is able to give to the specific abuse s/he has experienced. These games are healthy compensatory attempts to master the situation and should not be curtailed or interfered with.

As time passes, however, some children will enter new phases of reenacting the trauma in which—cognitively, emotionally, or behaviorally—they obsessively replay the traumatic event. Again, this may be part of the larger and healthy attempt to master their fears, but sometimes this mastery is not achieved, and children may stay preoccupied with painful memories of the event for years afterward. Over time, the event tends to become distorted and magnified in the child's mind. The child may even hallucinate various aspects of it, so by the time s/he discloses the trauma (again, as in cases of sexual abuse) years later in adulthood, the event has evolved into something different—and sometimes far more severe or terrifying—from what it was when it originally happened. This is the real danger of trauma: that children who are not able or encouraged to deal with its effects shortly after it occurs may be damaged by it internally and in some ways crippled by it for the rest of their lives. The life views of severely traumatized children are often badly altered—they may expect a future that is short-lived and void of many of the larger ambitions, curiosities, and feelings of aliveness more readily available to the child who has not been traumatized.

This means that it is essential for parents to recognize the symptoms of the child's reactions to traumatic stress. Post-traumatic stress disorder is the most common constellation of these symptoms, which tend to fall into one of three categories:

1. *Increased Arousal.* Children with this symptom tend to be irritable and angry and to overreact to minor frustrations with aggression and tantrums; they may also have trouble sleeping, and vigilantly protect their turf or watch warily over their environment to make sure it is safe. They are defensive, tend to startle easily, and generally are prey to various physiological or autonomic nervous system symptoms such as cardiovascular and intestinal reactions.

2. *Reexperiencing the Trauma.* The next group of symptoms is categorized by reliving the traumatic event, whether in nightmares, in repetitive play, or sometimes in the form of flashbacks.

3. *Avoidance and Dissociation.* The third group of symptoms is characterized by avoidance, numbness, and dissociation. Children with these symptoms avoid anything that reminds them (or triggers the memory) of

the traumatic event. They are frequently withdrawn, their feelings seem flat, and they tend to have a grim or pessimistic outlook. They may dissociate not only by appearing numb, depressed, or without emotion, but by fantasizing, depersonalizing (feeling unreal), losing all hope, becoming overly dependent, and sometimes exhibiting somatic symptoms such as fainting.

Post-traumatic stress disorder (PTSD) can and often does last for years and generally affects all aspects of life in very negative ways. Fortunately, some traumatized children may experience some of these symptoms for only a few weeks or months, after which they are able to move past them and gain some sort of mastery of their feelings; these children suffer not from PTSD but from what is called acute stress disorder. However, because the lifelong negative effects of PTSD can be so severe, parents need vigilantly to look out for signs of it so that their children, in the wake of trauma, may be helped to deal with its ramifications as quickly as possible—and heal to the point where they will not be negatively marked by the trauma for the rest of their lives.

WHAT TO DO

1. Because the subject of stress is so broad and complicated, it must be broken down into its component parts. For children who suffer from minor stresses, the source of stress should be relieved as soon as it is recognized to be causing problems. Most children occasionally suffer from what are called adjustment disorders, characterized by disturbances in their emotional, school, and social life that attend the normal frustrations of evolving from one stage of development to another. Parents are advised to soothe and help their children through these rough shoals. Ignoring the child's reactions to stress or insensitively

assuming the child should "tough it out" is rarely the best route. Parents also need to sensitize themselves to stress they may be causing the child, however unwittingly—such as forcing the child to be competitive at too early an age, or communicating unrealistic or perfectionistic expectations to the child. Give your children the help they need to relax—and move on.

2. For children exposed to overwhelmingly traumatic events, parents need first of all to be supportive and compassionate. Take measures to prevent the child from thinking s/he has caused the trauma in any way. This is particularly true in cases of sexual abuse, divorce, the death of a family member, accidents, being victimized by crime, or any type of natural disaster. Remember that very young children may not see the event logically—they may construct fantastic and self-blaming reasons for trauma that parents may not anticipate. Reassure your child that s/he is not to blame for circumstances out of his/her control.

3. Stay with your child and encourage him/her to draw, enact in games, and talk about the trauma in any way s/he pleases—repetitively if necessary, for days, weeks, and even months. Respect that children gain mastery according to their own timetables and cannot be expected to snap out of it, especially when reacting to a trauma they experience as overwhelming. The sooner and more completely the child is allowed to vent his/her feelings about the trauma, the less likely it is that the trauma will cause lifelong damage.

4. In the case of natural disasters that have affected many people, including children, parents should join the many support groups that generally arise in the community to gain the sense that they are not alone and to learn ways of coping with the disaster—including

ways of communicating with and reassuring children—
that may not have occurred to them.

5. If the child is afflicted by symptoms of PTSD for
   longer than a few weeks, professional help, in the form
   of individual, group, and/or family therapy, is certainly called for. Medication may also help, in the
   form of antidepressants, antianxiety agents, clonidine,
   and beta blockers, among others.

SEE ALSO

ANXIETY   CHILD PHYSICAL ABUSE
PSYCHOTROPIC MEDICATION   DEPRESSION
    AND CHILDREN   PSYCHOSOMATIC DISORDERS
SEXUAL ABUSE

CHAPTER THREE
Anger

"I don't care what Xena the Warrior Princess would do to your little brother if she were here, Caroline! Stop hitting him!"

Before (or maybe after) you laugh, think of the bind eight-year-old Caroline is in. She's mad at her little brother for crushing her watercolor paint box and thinks of the most rousing role model she can for how to get back at him: Xena the Warrior Princess. Boy, when Xena gets mad, you know it! She levels everyone in sight. "Isn't that a good thing, Mommy?"

The fact is, our culture sends wildly divergent messages about anger to all of us—but especially to our impressionable children. There's barely a Saturday morning cartoon that isn't based on surreal and lurid violence, with people exploding into bright purple, orange, and crimson bits. Clint Eastwood, Sylvester Stallone, Steven Seagal, Arnold Schwarzenegger, Jean-Claude Van Damme: These box-office winners have schooled us not only to expect violence in movies, but to slaver over it. At the same time, we are deluged with messages exhorting us to be peaceful, tolerate diversity, and accept everyone no matter who they are or what they do—from the Dalai Lama to Mr. Rogers and the Teletubbies, we're told to be sweet and gentle and noncompetitive. One parent complained to me: "My little boy switched from Barney on public TV to six men in a tag-team brawl on a cable TV broadcast of the WWF. What's he supposed to make of all that?"

Actually, that parent probably needn't fret. Most children

do not seem to be unduly bothered by the ambivalent messages about anger our culture blares at them. Parents worry,
often needlessly, that their children will be scarred or unable
to deal healthily with their own or others' anger because of
the violence they see on TV. The truth is that when children
have difficulty with anger, it's more usually because of what
they see going on in front of the TV. Their own families
teach them more about anger than Barney or Hulk Hogan
ever does. As a society, we seem to be terrified of anger. We
regard any expression of it as pathology—something automatically to be stamped out. In fact, anger is one of the
healthiest emotional states to which we have access. Anger is
a vivid signal to parents that something urgent inside of our
child needs attention.

Anger is as normal a feeling as joy, love, hunger, guilt,
shame, contentment, jealousy, anxiety, glee, and any number
of other normal emotions all children experience. I call
anger "the great communicator" because it signals so clearly
that help is needed. When that help arrives—usually in the
form of an attentive caregiver who is able to empathize with,
understand, and contain the child's anger—the anger goes
away. No harm is done. No scar is left. It is as if a great
windstorm subsides, and the child can go on without impediment to the next feeling, situation, state of being. The absence of anger is unnatural. If a parent tells me that his or
her child never gets angry, I ask him or her to bring in the
child for immediate consultation.

I define anger as a state of acute displeasure in response to
feelings of powerlessness or helplessness. There are two types
of anger. The first is developmental anger, which is anger
felt as the child moves through new and necessary adaptive
phases of development (such as toilet training), and which is
part of the child's process of mastery. There is also interpersonal anger, which arises from everyday normal interactions
with other people that cause momentary frustration: the "No,
you can't have another cookie—it's too close to dinner" type

of anger. This is the child's experience of other people not behaving the way s/he would like, and it can be very exasperating (many adults as well as children never fully or comfortably adapt to being frustrated). In the case of interpersonal anger, the child's needs and desires are often ignored or otherwise not met, and s/he gets angry. But this makes vivid what we need to understand about anger, which is that it is always a response to an underlying sense of felt helplessness or powerlessness at the moment.

However, the child's angry response varies with age and experience. In infants anger is expressed diffusely, in screams, crying, and sometimes the refusal or inability to feed well. The toddler who has just learned to walk now has a new arsenal to express anger: free hands. Suddenly able to grab spoons and balls and food and flowerpots, s/he discovers the power of throwing things in anger. Toddlers also exhibit stubbornness and learn the power of an angry "No!"—as in the "terrible twos" scenario. Toilet training happens at about this stage, and the toddler will also often display his or her anger in a refusal to use the bathroom. The preschool years, ages three to five, bring a greater array of physical skills and increased verbal ability, which add immensely to the child's weaponry. The toddler might have bitten in anger; the older child can now hit and kick and scratch and jump. Now instead of a sputtered angry "No!" we hear words like "I hate you!" or "Leave me alone!" or "You're the most horrible mother who ever lived!" Being accident prone, lying, or stealing can also be expressions of anger in the preschool stage. School presents a whole new arena in which to act out anger, and poor performance or disruptions in class, fighting in the cafeteria or on the playground, and truancy are common angry reactions of school-age kids. Anger can be hidden in more sophisticated guises as the child grows toward adolescence: Competitiveness and overambition frequently have their roots in anger.

We mishandle anger in many ways. Because many parents

are still often so uncomfortable with anger—our own as well as our children's—we may try to cover it up, pretend it's not there, or do anything else we can to deny it. We often don't see anger as normal because we haven't been educated to see it that way. When our children become angry, we may react by punishing them severely for displaying an emotion we were taught never to reveal. An angry child may seem "spoiled" because that's what we were always called when we got angry growing up. More complicated is our unconscious identification with an angry child—an identification that may frighten us. Harboring our own repressed angry feelings, we become terrified that we'll explode when we see our children "lose it." Losing control over anger may seem an intolerable prospect, and thus we will do anything we can to clamp down on our kids' expression of it. This also often means that we take our children's anger far more personally than we should, unable to handle the frequent "I hate you, Mommy and Daddy" that our little ones may yell at us. Children sometimes level criticism in anger that really cuts to the heart—even though the child's barb may be nothing more than a momentary howl of frustration, gone as quickly as it is expressed. We also may attempt to soothe an angry child because we are afraid of his or her anger; we may be overly compliant, even bribe the child to "be nice," and refuse to set necessary limits on the child's behavior. We might even try to eradicate anger with violent, hurtful responses of our own.

Mishandling a child's anger always leads to what I call "the anger metamorphosis." Prevented from expressing anger directly, the child represses it—and it then becomes a dangerous emotion, not a healthy one. Repressed anger metamorphoses into many psychiatric symptoms that may seem quite distant from anger but in fact are always caused by its repression. The popular notion of depression as anger turned inward is one clear example. But there are many more, and displaced hostilities, fears, and anxieties can plague the child not only through childhood but throughout the rest of his or her life. These legacies of mishandled anger are like the symptoms evinced by people who live around toxic waste dumps. The toxin stains and distorts everything, even if the symptoms may not seem to have been caused by it at all.

No one handles anger perfectly; perhaps in no other realm of child rearing does the phrase "progress, not perfection" have more currency. But we can do so much more as parents to encourage our children to express anger as anger—and show them by our ability to tolerate and contain it that they can learn to tolerate and contain it too.

WHAT TO DO

1. If your child truly gets out of control—throws things or becomes unmanageable, violent, or noisy—s/he is having what I call an anger emergency, which calls for anger first aid. Stay with the child, but restrain him or her in whatever way you must to avoid damage to the child or the environment, including other people. Do not shame the child. Do not separate from the child during this period. What you need to show the child is both that you are not afraid of his/her anger and that the anger will not be destructive. After this phase is over, proceed to the next suggestion.

2. Most anger is not uncontrolled, and anger first aid will not be necessary. Locating the trigger of the child's anger becomes the most important task, which generally means finding out why the child feels so powerless or helpless at this moment. Sometimes children will be able to tell you, but you will also be able to deduce for yourself from your child's patterns of angry behavior what their causes probably are. Sensitize yourself to normal developmental anger (a result of intestinal disturbance in infants, diapers that are

too tight, the crib tilted at an uncomfortable angle; or of frustrations in learning to walk, feeding him/herself, toilet training, first day of nursery school, dealing with a new sibling, etc.) and never take the child's expressions of anger personally. Where was your child before getting angry? Has there been a social, athletic, or educational stress? Is there an anxiety that has been creeping up? Remember that your child is probably experiencing angry reactions to completely normal frustrations and needs empathy and help.

3. Observe, listen to, and question your child compassionately if s/he is able to speak. Try not to criticize your child while attempting to discover what is bothering him or her.

4. Your primary goal is to relieve your child so that s/he can move beyond the anger without repressing or denying it. You might suggest a solution for a problem the child is facing (after you've allowed the child to express his or her anger about it; solutions given prematurely almost always increase anger, not decrease it). You might step in and give direct assistance (help with a frustrating task), provide indirect assistance (point out a self-defeating trend), or intervene in the environment (speak to an unfair teacher, call the school bully's parents). Most important (and difficult), you may have to take a hard look at yourself and the ways in which you may be contributing to your child's anger—and change your own behavior. This means not overly accommodating the child, but rather seeing what, if anything, you may be doing to exacerbate your child's anger. We need to remember that the major causes of interpersonal anger are some degree of unfairness, cold or neglectful treatment, not keeping promises, being inconsistent or hypocritical, inducing guilt, overprotecting, teasing, exercising

power arbitrarily, intimidation and humiliation, and even bullying your child. Being overly demanding, making unjust comparisons, and living vicariously through your child are all insidious ways we provoke our children to anger, and we parents need to sensitize ourselves to them so that we don't inflict them unwittingly on our kids. Remember most of all that you probably have prejudices against anger that need to be confronted and overcome in order to deal effectively with your children's anger. Unless your child's anger endangers him or her or the environment (which calls for anger first aid), focus on understanding rather than on lecturing or punishing your child. Realize that anger is a response to a terrible feeling of helplessness, and that once the source of its distress is located and acknowledged, it almost always dissipates on its own. If anger persists, you may need to seek professional counseling or therapy, such as that described in the chapter on behavior disorders.

SEE ALSO

BEHAVIOR DISORDERS	TANTRUMS
ANXIETY	STEALING
ALL TYPES OF THERAPY	LYING
PSYCHOTROPIC MEDICATION	FIGHTING
AND CHILDREN	ATTENTION DEFICIT DISORDER
FIRE SETTING	DISCIPLINE

CHAPTER FOUR

Anxiety

"What if the kids don't like me? What if the kids make fun of me? I hate this sweater, Mom, nobody's wearing dumb stuff like this! They'll think I'm a nerd. I don't feel well. Please don't make me go. . . ."

Anxiety may be the most ubiquitous emotional dilemma afflicting human beings, young or old. Nobody escapes feeling anxious at some points in life—typically when we face new situations, meet new people, grapple with new expectations. Distinct from depression or out-and-out fears and phobias, anxiety is evident from one major general symptom: worrying. Some children are bigger worriers than others, but no child completely escapes the affliction.

Anxiety rears its nervous head very early on. The good news is that, as with other uncomfortable emotional states, it often signals that the child has reached a new and important stage of development. An infant typically experiences stranger anxiety at about nine months; this is a welcome sign that the child has established a good solid bond with his/her major caretaker and is showing normal worry about losing that caretaker when new people come into his/her environment. It is equally normal for young children to worry about hurting themselves, or to feel apprehensive about new situations (going to school, to camp, or on vacation) or about the possible loss of a friend, parent, or pet. But by school age, perhaps the most common root of anxiety has to do with the child's fears about what others think about him/her.

Indeed, anxiety we may diagnose as pathological almost always turns out to be the product of a child's poor self-image—evident from excessive comparisons made to peers, and characterized by chronic jitteriness, intolerable phobias, and crippling fears of everyday situations. Anxiety at these times can manifest physically as shortness of breath, rapid heartbeat, diarrhea, nausea, shaking, skin rashes, sweating, headaches, sleeplessness, dizziness, and increased urination. The chronically anxious child will appear nervous, restless, tense. Sometimes, albeit rarely, the anxiety can become so great that the child experiences feelings of unreality. The anxious child is convinced s/he is constitutionally different from, "less than" his/her peers. Not surprisingly, such children feel helpless and unable to move out into the world. They often become secondarily depressed, house-bound, and overly attached to parents, and they are careful not to engage in any new behaviors that would threaten their fragile sense of security.

Children who chronically exhibit symptoms such as these are said to be suffering from generalized anxiety disorder, also referred to as overanxious disorder of childhood. Once again, children suffering from this disorder generally can be seen to be worriers—most commonly worrying about how others feel about them. They seek constant reassurance and approval from their parents (usually their mothers) and find it difficult to interact with others, especially other children— often alienating themselves from others with quick, panicky, and hostile reactions. They often appear perfectionistic, unable to tolerate even minor lapses in their or others' behavior, and they express scathing self-criticism and negative comparisons between themselves and their peers.

Predictably, such children often come from very demanding families—home environments in which they feel pressured to behave according to strict rules or standards. Failure is not tolerated in such families; praise for accomplishment is rare. Fortunately, most children eventually outgrow the poor self-concepts they grapple with in these family situations, learning simply in the process of growing up that they need not be so hard on themselves or others. Others are scarred much more deeply, and may need professional help.

WHAT TO DO

1. It may seem ironic that a child suffering from generalized anxiety disorder often tends to rule the family he/she feels is ruling him/her. Others may feel they have to walk on eggshells around a child who is prone to anxiety attacks. In such cases, it is important to establish sensible boundaries and limits on the child's behavior—to let the child know his/her anxiety will not dictate the behavior of the entire household.

2. It is essential that the family also look as honestly as possible at their own behaviors and impacts on the anxious child. Often nervous and high-strung children are reflections of their parents' equally nervous and high-strung personalities—cranked up to an extreme. Many parents are thus blind to their own contributions to their children's anxiety; to such parents, it's "normal" to be perfectionistic or to worry continually about other people's opinions. It is difficult for any of us to admit that we may have destructively pressured our children to behave in certain ways—imposing our own standards on children whose temperaments and talents and desires may in fact be very different from our own.

3. If a child's anxiety does not improve over time, it is usually necessary for the entire family to enter treatment together so that they can awaken to the sometimes destructive modes of interaction they may not know they are perpetuating. Family therapy is perhaps the mainstay of treatment for this disorder. Other forms of therapy that have proven useful are forms of cognitive behavioral therapy, relaxation technique

therapy, and the use of antianxiety medication. However, prescribing tranquilizers to children is something generally to be wary of: Side effects such as drowsiness, feelings of mild intoxication, interference with memory and other cognitive skills, and the possibility of addiction argue against taking this recourse. Attending to the root cause through family therapy—the impact of the family on the anxious child—is almost always the better path to healing.

SEE ALSO

FEARS AND PHOBIAS
SCHOOL PHOBIA
SEPARATION ANXIETY
STRESS
DEPRESSION AND
   MANIA

PSYCHOTROPIC MEDICATION
   AND CHILDREN
ALL TYPES OF THERAPY
THE UNDERACHIEVER
OBSESSIVE-COMPULSIVE
   DISORDER

CHAPTER FIVE

Fears and Phobias

"I don't wanna take swimming lessons anymore, Mom. Please don't make me! They're gonna teach us how to dive next, and I don't wanna do it. I'm scared of going in head-first. I can't do it! Please, Mom? I can swim already—I don't need to learn anything else. . . ."

"I won't go into the water. You can't make me. Nothing can make me. You can punish me all you want, but I won't go into the water. I won't. That's it."

The resistant children I've quoted here are both grappling with fear—but fears of quite different intensity. The first child has been able to deal with the challenge of learning how to swim but feels stuck at the new lesson his swimming class is going to tackle next. Nearly every child in the world will feel tripped up now and then about having to learn something unfamiliar—being scared is a normal reaction. With sympathy and reassurance and compassionate coaxing, a parent will generally be able to help the child overcome this fear and at least attempt the behavior that frightens him or her. Such attempts eventually prove to the child that fears can be faced and worked through.

But the second child experiences fear of a different order—a fear strong and intractable enough to be labeled a phobia. Phobias are quite a different species from more everyday fears and anxieties; they always symbolize some deeper dilemma that the child is battling unconsciously, and thus require a different order of understanding and treatment.

FEARS—WHAT TO DO ABOUT THEM

First, let's look at what we can do to help your child grapple with the far more common variety of "being scared" fear he or she inevitably will encounter in the everyday process of growing up.

1. It's important that you take your child's fears seriously, even though you may realize rationally that they are nothing to be afraid of.

2. Don't panic. Fear is contagious: If you react to your child's fear by becoming afraid yourself, you'll just sustain the problem.

3. Don't get angry at your child for being afraid. This will simply increase your child's fear of you and make it more difficult for him/her to tell you what's causing the fear.

4. Don't force your child to confront the source of his/her fear immediately. Making little Donna go out to the raft anyway and learn how to dive before you've given her a chance to talk about it and calm down will just make matters worse. Most fears go away on their own; give the child a chance to calm down and perhaps reason herself out of her fear.

5. Help your child by reassuring her/him that fears of all types are absolutely normal. All people have them. You may want to read them stories about other children who have been scared and how they overcame it (many such books are available at the library or in your local bookstore). Perhaps you can also talk about a fear of your own and how you dealt with it.

PHOBIAS—WHAT TO DO ABOUT THEM

For some children fears become very marked and don't go away on their own—or even with the help we've described above. The child will do everything possible to avoid any encounter with what causes the fear, and no amount of reassurance or rational argument helps to lessen the fear. These intransigent fears are called phobias—irrational fears of situations, activities, and/or people the child encounters every day that most other people don't experience with such intensity or abhorrence. Avoidance becomes the hallmark of the phobic child's life, and it can take very extreme forms. Phobias commonly center on dogs, insects, loud noises, snakes, cats, water, the dark, monsters, ghosts, blood, fire, germs, strangers, being alone, heights, being closed in (claustrophobia), crowds, or walking on the street or other open spaces (agoraphobia), among many others.

Phobias always signal that something deeper is troubling the child than the manifest trigger (cats, dogs, strangers, monsters, etc.) indicates on its own. The source of the phobia is always symbolic: There is always some underlying anxiety that is displaced onto the thing the child is conscious of fearing. For example, fear of dogs may really cover a deeper guilty fear of expressing anger to a parent. A fear of open spaces may relate to a deeper fear of being abandoned by a parent. The usually oblique connections to these underlying fears are what make phobias so challenging to deal with, for nothing is as it seems on the surface. There is always something else going on underneath.

The main task is to help the child become less frightened of his/her inner life: to learn that s/he will not be abandoned or punished for angry or guilty thoughts, and to give the child more of a sense of unconditional love. This must nearly always be done in stages, particularly if the phobia is severe enough to disrupt the child's and the family's life. First everything must be done to calm the anxiety as quickly as possible to prevent further complications, such as disruptions in school or at home. Second, the child must be helped to understand the displacements he/she is making and brought gently to confront the real deep-seated fear beneath the phobia, and thus to develop better ways to cope. Last, the family must be ruthlessly honest about its own contributions to that deeper fear and change its modes of interaction with the phobic child.

It is also important to remember that phobias sometimes come from trauma. In other words, a child may have had a horrible experience, either directly or vicariously—such as witnessing a death, being mugged or robbed or molested, or hearing accounts of violence on television or at school, among many others—that may not seem to the parent always to warrant such an extreme response, but which triggers an entrenched phobia in the child. These phobias—what I call traumatic phobias—are not necessarily displaced from a more underlying fear. Often enabling the child to articulate the trauma is enough to rid the child of the phobia.

In summary, here's what to do if your child is phobic:

1. Understand that, like normal fears, most phobias clear up on their own with common sense and compassionate attention on the part of parents.

2. If your own attempts to reassure the child and get him/her to explore the anxieties and fears that underlie the phobia fail, professional help may be necessary. Expect the mental health professional you consult to investigate possible events or behaviors in the household that may have led to unresolved issues to which the child gives expression through his/her phobia. The focus will be to relieve the child's anxiety while at the same time trying to understand what is causing it. Some form of psychotherapy—individual and/or family—is usually indicated, as well as the possible use of medication, including tranquilizers and some antidepressants. One form of psychotherapy in the treatment of phobias that is quite popular is cognitive behavioral therapy, which helps the child deal directly with the feared situation and often bypasses the need

to look for "deeper" psychic causes of the child's distress. This is an approach that predictably works best in the case of phobias caused by readily identifiable traumas.

3. Remember that even though your child's phobias may strike you as "silly" or "unreal," they have tremendous crippling force to your child, and must always be taken seriously. They can become disabling to the child throughout his/her life if they are not treated with compassion and understanding and, where indicated, responsible professional help. Don't let the phobia persist without treatment for too long. If it lasts for longer than several weeks to a month, and the child does not become less phobic as a result of your own compassionate care, seek professional help.

SEE ALSO

ANXIETY   ALL TYPES OF THERAPY
STRESS   PSYCHOTROPIC MEDICATION
SEPARATION ANXIETY   AND CHILDREN
SCHOOL PHOBIA

CHAPTER SIX

Separation Anxiety

"But what if you and Daddy get into an accident? What if your car drives off the road? What if you never come back? Don't go—please don't go. . . . I'll be good, Mommy— stay home and I won't make any trouble—I'm sorry. Don't leave me!"

What we call growing up might be seen as the product of learning to tolerate new separations from our parents and other loved ones, departing from the familiar and developing the courage to embark on new adventures and interact with new people in unfamiliar situations. From the moment we emerge from the safety of the womb, we begin to discover what is "me" and "not me." No infant or child likes the idea that Mommy and Daddy and the rest of the world are different from him/her, or "not me." To varying degrees, we all resist the idea of separation, and the fears and anxieties we experience as we encounter new separations are completely normal.

When a child is nine months old, the unfamiliar might take the form of strangers—people other than Mommy and Daddy in whose presence the infant feels anxious. This fear of strangers is a normal and healthy sign that the infant has formed a strong bond with his or her parents: Fearing the bond might be broken is a testament to the strength of the child's strong attachment to Mommy and Daddy. Anxieties about starting school, going to camp, or moving to a new town and making new friends are all also perfectly normal. They ultimately induce the child to confront new fears of separation and take the risk to form new bonds, as well as develop new ideas about how to operate in a larger and less predictable world.

Sometimes, however, separation from parents causes severe worry—even panic—to the point that the whole household becomes disrupted and badly stressed. Children who experience extreme or intolerable separation anxiety typically come from close-knit families in which strangers or anything new is mistrusted: The child gets the idea that the larger world is dangerous and that the only safe place is home. In other words, children with great anxieties about being separated from their homes or families often have parents who themselves suffer separation anxiety. Other risk factors increasing the likelihood that a child will experience high separation anxiety include dealing with the severe illness or death of a family member, divorce, or other dramatic disruptions of family structure, such as moving too many times or into too many unfamiliar neighborhoods and/or cultural venues (e.g., "army brats" who move dozens of times in childhood). Other children who seem particularly prone to separation anxiety are those with developmental problems in learning or attention deficit disorder and children who are chronically ill and in need of greater-than-usual parental care.

Separation anxiety may be mild—for example, nervous anticipation of parents going out for an evening, or fears of going to sleep. When mild, these anxieties generally respond to warm parental reassurance and measures such as making sure the child has a baby-sitter s/he knows and likes when the parents go out, installing a night-light, or indulging in comforting nighttime rituals (such as reading a favorite bedtime story) when the child goes to sleep.

However, for other children separation anxiety can be quite severe. The prospect of going to camp, to school, or even to sleep can bring on fears of panic proportions. Such children often manifest their anxiety with physical symptoms such as stomachaches, headaches, palpitations, nausea, and vomiting. Sometimes the mere mention of a parent leaving is enough to cause such severe reactions as the inability to sleep, obsessive fixations on imagined catastrophes that will befall the parent if s/he leaves the house, clinging to Mommy and Daddy, or trying to be the "perfect child" so that the parent won't want to leave. Parents feed into this anxiety sometimes by becoming terribly anxious themselves, so when they do leave the home on a shopping expedition or to go to work, they may not be able to function well because of worrying about the emotional state of the child they've left at home. The problem quickly becomes a family problem: As the child's disability grows, parents and siblings can't help but become affected by the child's growing distress, and the life of the entire household is badly disrupted.

Separation anxiety is to be expected to some degree in all children under the age of five or six. Of course, there is wide variety in what may be considered "normal." As always, the child's individual temperament plays a strong role in how distressed he or she may feel at any stage of development about the prospect of separating from Mommy and Daddy: Some children are needier than others, more or less prone to taking risks, and so on. In the majority of cases, no matter what the degree of resistance to change, children navigate these crises and learn to survive separation—and move on to the next stage of development without lasting problems. However, whether mild or severe, the family's reactions to the child's distress is of seminal importance. Family members need to see whether they are fostering a fear of separation via their own fears and behaviors, as well as to provide necessary boundaries and reassurances that will help the child to overcome his or her own fears of separation. The following suggestions are geared to help parents accomplish this.

WHAT TO DO WHEN
SEPARATION ANXIETY IS MILD

1. Expect separation anxiety to be present at nearly all stages of a child's life, diminishing as the child gets to elementary school but always reemerging at moments in which the child moves toward independence.

2. Be patient with and present for young children. Prepare them for anticipated separations—for example, being clear that bedtime is half an hour away, or that a trip is coming up where one parent will accompany the child but the other won't. When taking your child for the first time to nursery school, stay until you see that the child has begun to participate in group activities. If you can, be available by phone so that the child can contact you at periods of greatest stress and need. Sometimes giving your child a snapshot of you will assuage his or her fears. Remember that separation anxiety is normal and your sympathetic presence and reassurance are vitally important in achieving resolution. Remember also that by elementary school, and certainly by preadolescence, there is generally no cause for concern: The child will have worked through this anxiety her- or himself. But perhaps above all, don't foist too much independence or enforce too strong a "stiff upper lip" stance on your child. Your child needs to come back to you and break away from you at his or her own pace. Be sensitive to your child's needs for reassurance and independence, and respond accordingly.

WHAT TO DO WHEN SEPARATION
ANXIETY IS MORE SEVERE

1. The most important task confronting the parents of a child who experiences severe separation anxiety is to

be ruthlessly honest with themselves in the course of a careful self-examination. Are you reinforcing your child's fears by conveying that all risks are too dangerous to take and that home is the only safe place for the child to be? Do you cling too closely to your own child, not encouraging him or her to play with friends or engage in extracurricular activities at school? Does the child see you talk to your own parents too much on the phone, depending on them now as much as you may have done in childhood? These are difficult questions to answer on your own, and individual therapy for you may be necessary to confront and fully acknowledge the answers. In addition, family therapy can help engage you and your child in the pursuit of more independent lives.

2. Children who experience severe separation anxiety benefit from a structured approach to getting better. They need praise for any steps forward they take. Map out the day for your child and make sure s/he knows when s/he's expected to go to the playground or to school and when Mommy or Daddy may have to go to work or out shopping. Reassure the child at every point that s/he will be safe and that you and s/he will reunite at a specific time. Rehearse what it will be like when you go out and your child goes to bed. Make sure your child feels comfortable with the baby-sitter. The key here is calm anticipation. Help the child realize not only that his or her behavior will help to get him/her through temporary separations but that the child will be helping the whole family to be happier and more at ease.

3. If reassurance, rehearsals, and the passage of time don't improve the child's anxiety, then professional consultation should be sought. After ruling out the more rare possible causes of anxiety—physical afflictions such

as migraine headaches or stomach and bowel disorders, mental conditions such as chronic depression, developmental disorders, schizophrenia, and other anxiety disorders—the focus of treatment will be to decrease the child's anxiety so that s/he can go to school or function better in day-to-day activities. Family and individual therapy (for both parent and child) may be called for, as well as cognitive behavioral therapy for shorter-term treatment. In particularly severe cases such therapy may be combined with medications such as imipramine, Paxil, Prozac, and Zoloft, or anti-anxiety agents such as Klonopin and Ativan.

SEE ALSO

ANXIETY

DEPRESSION AND MANIA

FEARS AND PHOBIAS

PSYCHOTROPIC MEDICATION
    AND CHILDREN

ALL TYPES OF THERAPY

SCHOOL PHOBIA

PERVASIVE DEVELOPMENTAL
    DISORDER

SCHIZOPHRENIA

PSYCHOSOMATIC DISORDERS

CHAPTER SEVEN

Grief

"But where did Grandma go? She went to heaven? Where's that? What do you mean, she's never coming back?"

It's probably not news to you that in our society, death is a more taboo topic than even the more lurid extremes of sex or violence. Typically we shield our children from any unpleasant encounter with it—or try to. I can't count the number of times parents have asked me whether their children should be allowed to attend a funeral, view a dead body, attend a wake, or even be told about the death of a dear relative. As adults, we may give lip service to the idea that death is a natural part of life, but few of us seem to convey that message to our kids when Grandma or Aunt Clara or Uncle George or Cousin Stevie dies. We often feel as ill-equipped to handle death—and are as terrified of it—as we tend to make our children.

While it's not surprising that we tend to visit our own anxieties about death onto our children, it's important to wake up to the fact that we do this so that we can take measures to stop doing it. From early on in childhood, children should be afforded the opportunity to learn that death is indeed a natural part of life. If parents point out the cycles of the seasons—buds in spring turning to leaves, which then naturally age and die in fall and winter—even very young children can begin to appreciate nature's ongoing cycle of life and death, and start to see every living thing's place in that cycle. However, parents also need to realize that the capacity to register the facts of death changes depending on the child's maturity. For children of preschool age, death may be viewed simply as going to sleep or traveling somewhere. As the child

grows through the school-age years, his/her capacity to understand death similarly grows. The child will first understand
death as something that happens to others; by the age of eight,
s/he will begin to see that its finality applies to him- or herself as well. By the end of the elementary school years—the
beginning of preadolescence—nearly all children understand
and can accept the finality of death, although, of course, different children feel varying degrees of ease in accepting it.
They may even express the desire to be dead themselves in order to join a lost loved one. This should not automatically be
confused with suicidal despair; it's often a normal expression
of mourning the loved one they've lost. (Of course, if this
thought is accompanied by suicidal actions or is part of a
larger picture of depression, then it has more significance.)

In addition to sadness and yearning to be with the person
who has died, other normal reactions in children to death may
include such physical symptoms as problems with sleeping (insomnia, nightmares, etc.), headaches, intestinal disturbances,
and loss of appetite. Symptoms may mirror those of chronic
depression but should not automatically be thought to be evidence of it. A period of mourning is normal and healthy and
does not indicate the necessity of intervening in the ways that
chronic depression calls for, even when the child expresses
what may at first seem like alarming ideas: for example, hallu-
cinating the dead person's presence, or not believing that the
person has died. As dramatic as these distortions are, they indicate the child's attempts to make sense of something very
disturbing, and they are often completely normal transitional
adaptations to the death. Indeed, we often hear about these
same sorts of ideas from adults, and we don't leap to diagnose
them as abnormal. It is normal for some children to react to
death with great anger, problems concentrating in school, and
withdrawal from social activities. Some children feel guilt and
may provoke other people into anger so that they can be
"punished" for what they secretly feel they've caused.

What about the child who loses a parent? Most people be-

lieve that this must scar the child for life. However, the literature does not bear this out. Studies are quite inconclusive
about the effects of a parent's death on a child, but they do indicate how important the quality of care is after that death, either from the surviving spouse or from others in the family or
community who take on that care. We also know that a very
young child who loses a parent will need particularly close and
intensive attention. Predictably, fewer problems are experienced by children who have not had an unusually conflicted
relationship with the parent who has died. If the parent dies
after an illness that the child has known about, the child's transition through the grief stage is made easier: The death will
make more sense because of the illness that preceded it. However, most important is the emotional state of the surviving
spouse or caretaker. How depressed or unavailable to the child
this caretaker may be will have a strong impact on the child's
own ease or difficulty in working through his or her grief.

WHAT TO DO

1. Depending on the age of the child, the parent should
   make an effort to include him or her in discussions of
   the death and funeral arrangements. Answer all of the
   child's questions as simply and warmly as possible.

2. Friends as well as family members need to be as sympathetic as possible to the child and should never dismiss what may seem to be irrational, angry, or even
   hallucinatory reactions the child may have.

3. Morbid discussions about the disease process as well as
   involved supernatural explanations are not appropriate
   for children of preschool age.

4. Very young children's curiosity about the death process
   is often satisfied simply by saying that various parts of
   the body have stopped functioning—a bit like a ma-
   chine running down.

5. Take advantage of the many books on children and grieving that you'll find in libraries and bookstores. Some suggestions are *The Grieving Child: A Parent's Guide*, by H. Fitzgerald and E. Kübler-Ross; *Talking About Death: A Dialogue Between Parent and Child*, by E. Grollman and S. Avishai; and *Talking with Children About Loss: Words, Strategies and Wisdom to Help Children Cope with Death, Divorce and Other Difficult Times*, by M. Trozzi and K. Massimini.

6. If reactions to grief seem abnormally acute or persistent, the parent should certainly investigate the possibility of professional intervention. Serious and intractable guilt, severe relational problems, intense feelings of shame, suicidal thoughts or actions, and dramatic weight loss all may indicate a serious depression requiring treatment—generally individual and family therapy, and sometimes antidepressant medication.

7. There are many grief support groups available for the child and his/her family.

8. Perhaps most important is that parents assess their own approaches to and attitudes about death. Children follow our lead nowhere more than in our attitudes about death and our own capacity to accept its inevitability: We do them as well as ourselves the best service when we make sure our own attitudes about death and dying are as healthy as possible.

SEE ALSO

DEPRESSION AND MANIA   PSYCHOTROPIC MEDICATION
STRESS   AND CHILDREN
THE UNDERACHIEVER   ALL TYPES OF THERAPY
SEPARATION ANXIETY

CHAPTER EIGHT

Obsessive-Compulsive Disorder

"Step on a crack, you'll break your mother's back! Step on a line, you'll break your father's spine!"

Few children are not convinced at some point that they must adhere to ritualistic or repetitive behaviors to protect themselves or, as in the rhymes quoted above, other people in their lives. Preschool-age children may line up their stuffed animals in a very precise order, according to size or color or type of beast, and won't go to sleep until the ritual is satisfactorily completed. Wearing the right clothes exactly in the right way may be the child's condition for leaving the house and going off to kindergarten: "No, Mommy, I have to wear the blue sweater over the pink shirt!" As irrational as these conditions may seem to adults, they assume huge importance to the child for a simple reason: They give the child some sense of control over an environment that would otherwise be intolerably bewildering. Children have very little power over their lives when they are young, and forming and adhering to certain rituals gives them a sense that they're not entirely the victims of adult decisions or incomprehensible circumstances. Children tend to discard these ritualistic or compulsive behaviors as they grow and develop more adult ways of asserting themselves and wielding power in the world; generally, by the beginning of elementary school they are gone almost completely. However, when a child's development hits a bump in the road—when something happens to frighten the child or make her/him feel powerless again—

it's not surprising for the ritual to reappear: The thumb goes back in the mouth, the blue sweater must be worn over the pink shirt, and the little girl or boy would sooner die than step on a crack in the sidewalk.

For very anxious children, these ritual thoughts and behaviors become obsessions and compulsions. Obsession has to do with an unwanted thought, image, or impulse that the child may realize is senseless, unnecessary, and intrusive but whose repetition the child cannot control. Actually, it's important to remember that many children in the grip of an obsession don't understand its senselessness, for to them, it's incontrovertible truth. A compulsion has to do with the activity or behavior in which the child engages in reaction to an obsession—an activity resorted to because of a perceived internal obligation, often to protect the child him- or herself or to guard a family member or friend. The obsession in "Step on a crack, you'll break your mother's back" is the child's belief that his or her own ritual behavior may harm his/her mother if he/she is not careful what steps he/she takes; the compulsion is therefore not to step on that crack. As you may intuit from even this simple example, the internal obligation the child feels isn't simply to spare his/her mother by walking a certain way down the sidewalk; more deeply, it may well be to protect Mommy from angry impulses the child does not wish to believe he or she has. In other words, obsessive-compulsive behavior is almost always more complicated than it first appears. It often is an intricate defense that the child resorts to because he/she feels there is no other choice. Rarely does obsession occur without a correlative compulsion; the two go hand in hand.

When these rituals become truly obsessive-compulsive, they shackle the child in many unfortunate ways and can have a devastating impact on the whole household as well. A child who can only use his or her left hand to turn on a light, who must wash his or her hands twelve times every time s/he passes the bathroom, who will not eat anything red or green or white, who will not wear anything that hasn't been ironed six times—well, it's easy to sympathize with the parent who thinks such a child may have gone completely around the bend. Many studies about different aspects of obsessive-compulsive disorder (OCD) are currently under way, and the genesis of this disorder is still very much shrouded in mystery. There is evidence that genetic factors may be involved, as well as possible constitutional defects in the body's use of neurotransmitters such as serotonin, norepinephrine, and dopamine; there is even some evidence of morphological conditions in the brain similar to those of Parkinson's disease. A majority of children recover from the disorder to some degree, but the condition does seem to wane and wax for many people throughout their lifetimes, and a small percentage do not improve at all. About all that can be said categorically is that children who suffer from obsessive-compulsive disorder are very nervous children indeed. And that, finally, suggests the best and most effective route of treatment.

WHAT TO DO

1. Keep in mind that whatever pain or discomfort the obsessive-compulsive child may cause the family, his or her own self-torture is usually far worse. With a child in the grip of this kind of repetitive thinking and behavior, compassion is always the best first approach. Remember that the condition may well cure itself if the child is not unduly punished for a transgression s/he truly does not feel s/he can control.

2. Parents should also keep in mind that there are many other psychiatric disorders that exhibit features and symptoms similar to those of obsessive-compulsive disorder, and they should not jump to conclusions about any diagnosis until various alternatives have been ruled out by a professional. These include chronic depression,

phobias, post-traumatic stress disorder, schizophrenia, Tourette's syndrome, and psychosomatic disorders (all of which are covered in other chapters in this book).

3. It has been found sometimes that excessively giving in to the obsessive-compulsive child can increase family anger and ends up being more destructive to the child. It also may reinforce the behavior as an effective attention-getting tactic—which, once again, just causes more resentment in the rest of the family and makes it less likely that the child will give up the behavior. In other words, resisting the behavior is often better in the long run for both child and family as long as that resistance takes place in the context of genuine empathy and continuing attempts to understand the obsessive-compulsive child's distress.

4. Professional help is usually a must. The professional will be able to rule out any psychiatric problems with symptoms that may overlap those of this disorder and also be able to prescribe the correct treatment.

5. Treatment usually includes individual psychotherapy; various cognitive and behavioral interventions have proven effective as well. Family therapy and support will also more than likely be necessary.

6. Psychotropic medications have become part and parcel of modern treatment of OCD. Medications such as Anafranil, Prozac, Luvox, and Zoloft are presently the most common ones. They tend to decrease the obsessive-compulsive symptoms and bring some relief for everyone.

SEE ALSO

DEPRESSION AND MANIA

FEARS AND PHOBIAS

SCHIZOPHRENIA

PERVASIVE DEVELOPMENTAL
    DISORDER (AUTISM)

PSYCHOTROPIC MEDICATION
    AND CHILDREN

RITUALS

ALL TYPES OF THERAPY

STRESS

TICS (INCLUDING TOURETTE'S
    SYNDROME)

CHAPTER NINE
The Hypochondriac

"I'm sick, Mommy, I really am. My tummy hurts and my head feels funny. I can't go to school today. Please don't make me. I'm really sick. . . ."

Mommy takes Billy's temperature again and it's perfectly normal. His head is cool. He looks fine. What is he trying to get out of this time? How seriously should she take his complaints? Should she call the doctor? Or will it turn out to be like the last time, and the doctor will say there's nothing wrong—except maybe Billy's attitude about going to school?

Hypochondriasis isn't something we generally associate with children, except in the above classic case of a child trying to get out of doing something s/he doesn't want to do. However, at a time when the media, from TV to the Internet, bombard us with dire warnings about strange new diseases, when we're told we can get sick from hamburgers or eggs, new strains of tuberculosis, AIDS, and ever-mutating flu viruses, the incidence of hypochondriasis in children as well as adults seems to be rising. Children's imaginations often run wild about possible illnesses they may have. One little boy, about eight years old, told me that he was sure he had "air disease": "Contaminants" (he used that word; he'd heard it on *60 Minutes*) in the air were flooding his cells with toxins. He wanted his mother to give him a mask to filter out the bad air so he wouldn't be sick. Another girl of nine was sure she had a virus that caused headaches, making her miss days of school at a time and undergo endless expensive medical tests, none of which revealed any physical cause, but all of which badly disrupted her life and the lives of her family members. Hypochondriasis is no fun for hypochondriacs or the families who must attend to them.

Physical complaints should never be taken lightly, and certainly any child who complains of pain, bodily distress, or an illness that does not go away should be examined by a doctor. When no physical cause can be isolated or diagnosed, however, it's safe to assume that the complaint is a symbolic one: The child in effect hides behind a physical complaint, much as s/he may hide behind certain ritualistic behaviors or obsessive-compulsive disorders, to express fear or anger or discomfort s/he doesn't know how to express in any other way. The deeper and less conscious problem is displaced by worries about physical symptoms or illness—and the displacement can be very entrenched. It's virtually impossible to reason a hypochondriac out of his/her hypochondria, as the child's attachment to the imaginary illness is unconscious and quite fiercely defended.

We are not sure why certain children become hypochondriacal and others do not. Certainly a child who grows up in a household in which siblings or parents are or have been very sick have a model of illness that they may take on because they can see it attracts concern and attention. Indeed, children may become very jealous of siblings who are "always sick"—and wish the sickness upon themselves so that they can assume a more central place in the family.

WHAT TO DO

1. First of all, remember that hypochondriacs get sick too. Take your child's complaints seriously and have a good pediatrician rule out any physical cause for these complaints.

2. As with rituals and obsessions and compulsions, if a child's complaints prove to be hypochondriacal, they should not be allowed to rule the life of the family. It is important to set limits and provide structure for the

hypochondriacal child: Express sympathy but also lay down the law about chores, the necessity of going to school even if the child doesn't feel perfectly well, and so on. In the long run, pandering to the hypochondriacal child not only reinforces his or her use of hypochondriasis as an attention-getting tactic, but it increases the family's own anger and resentment toward the child. Be firm about behavior you will not tolerate, even as you express concern about the child's health and well-being.

3. Most cases of hypochondriasis go away by preadolescence, but if your child continues to complain of imaginary illnesses for longer than several weeks, professional help may be indicated. The mental health professional will rule out other psychiatric syndromes that may have hypochondriacal symptoms (such as anxiety disorders, depression, obsessive-compulsive disorder, psychosomatic disorders, separation anxiety disorder, school phobia, and, far more rarely, psychotic disorders). Individual and family therapy will generally help to ease the hypochondriac's symptoms, as will, in most cases, the simple passage of time.

4. Hypochondriacs' worries rarely occur in isolation. They are usually part of other syndromes, and the treatment for those other syndromes will usually eradicate hypochondriacal symptoms as a matter of course.

SEE ALSO

ANXIETY

DEPRESSION AND MANIA

RITUALS

SEPARATION ANXIETY

PSYCHOSOMATIC DISORDERS

OBSESSIVE-COMPULSIVE
     DISORDER

SOCIAL PHOBIA

SCHIZOPHRENIA

BEHAVIOR

CHAPTER TEN
Tantrums

If you're consulting this chapter, you've very likely already looked at the chapter on anger. If so, you know that, far from being automatic evidence of pathology, anger is a very important and effective communicator, especially for young children who may not be able to verbalize or have any perspective about the frustration they feel. Anger is a response to a feeling of helplessness: When we see an angry child, we see a child crying out to be heard, understood, and reassured.

Most angry children are not out of control. However, if anger does get out of control, it frequently takes the form of tantrums. There may be no more vexing situation for a parent than having to deal with a child throwing a tantrum (screaming, red in the face, limbs flailing) at home, in a shopping mall, at a restaurant, or at the in-laws' house. In fact, the most frequently asked question parents ask me about their children's anger is "How do I control the tantrums?"—largely because of their embarrassment at their kids throwing tantrums in public.

Tantrums are most frequent in very young children, beginning in infancy and often cropping up when the child is two (those "terrible twos" often *are* terrible because of tantrums) or three. Most children under the age of three who have tantrums do not grow up to exhibit excessively aggressive or destructive behavior. However, if tantrums persist after age three and four, there is reason for concern: Studies do show that these children tend to have more difficulty handling their anger later in life.

A tantrum is a signal that a child momentarily feels overwhelmed by a sense of powerlessness, which results in rage. This suggests two important facts about tantrums that every parent is well advised to remember: (1) A child does not plan temper tantrums; they should not be seen as calculated attempts to annoy parents, and (2) when a child throws a tantrum, s/he is truly out of control; you cannot reason a child out of a tantrum.

Like anger, tantrums most frequently arise either from frustration at not feeling able to manage a task associated with normal development (learning to walk is the clearest example of this) or from interpersonal interactions in which the child does not get what s/he wants from another person ("No, you can't have a cookie before dinner"). Not surprisingly, children who are hungry, tired, or physically ill are more prone to tantrums than children who are not.

However, whatever their cause, tantrums require a quick response from parents, who need to employ tactics that may be very different from measures they take to deal with other, less volatile forms of anger.

WHAT TO DO

1. The first step in handling a tantrum is to realize that the child is out of control and that you cannot take the tantrum personally. It is not the product of any conscious attempt on the child's part to embarrass you.

2. The practice of what I call anger first aid is almost always called for when a child has a tantrum. This is not the time to look for causes; to ensure the safety of the child, others, and the environment, you usually need physically to stop the tantrum. This may mean holding and restraining the child so s/he does not bang his/her head, throw tuna cans in the supermarket, kick the checkout clerk, or fall out of a high chair. Holding may then become cradling until the tantrum runs its course and the child is soothed and calms

down. Some children may hold their breath during a tantrum; while this may scare the daylights out of a parent, be assured that the child *will* breathe again when s/he has to. If the tantrum occurs at home, some children prefer to be left alone; if there are no objects that the child can use to damage the environment or him/herself, this may be a good idea.

3. Remember that tantrums usually are limited bursts of anger and run their course fairly quickly. They are then followed by a slow but steady reversion back to normality. During the heat of a tantrum, parents should hold and stay with the child, and not lecture, cajole, or have much verbal interchange. Tantrums are not the time to talk.

4. After the tantrum is completely over, you need to sit down with your child and discuss the reason for the out-of-control behavior. For children who are capable of verbal exchanges, this means finding out what the trigger might have been. Let the child talk; this is not the moment for recriminations. Often just venting his or her remaining anger about the trigger is enough to lessen that anger. For infants who don't yet talk, the parent must examine what happened right before the tantrum to trigger it and see, if possible, that it doesn't happen again.

5. Possibly most important is that the parent not lose control when the child does. If it seems that you will react with your own uncontrollable anger, relegate the child to someone else's care at that moment if possible.

6. Do not bribe a child out of a tantrum. This simply teaches the child that a tantrum is currency, a way of getting what s/he wants. Similarly, a child should never be rewarded for a tantrum. For example, if a child has a tantrum because you will not give him or her a piece of candy, do not give the child candy after

the tantrum. Let your child know you are not afraid of his or her tantrums; this not only gives the child the sense that his or her anger is containable and manageable, but also helps you to set reasonable limits on the child's behavior.

7. Give your child latitude and a range of choices when you can, particularly if you know that certain situations or verbal disagreements will trigger tantrums. For example, if your child typically responds to change by having a tantrum, make sure you announce well in advance that the change is coming. When possible, do not engage in oppositional verbal battles with your child if they trigger tantrums. Let your child win an argument or debate—it does no harm, and it will increase his or her sense of power. Give your child choices. For example, if it's cleanup time, say s/he can do it now, or five minutes from now, or even later that afternoon. Allow your child to choose from several clothing options what to wear that day.

8. Understanding what has triggered the tantrum is far more important than punishing the child for having it. If you decide on punishment, make sure it is meted out well after the tantrum has occurred and after you have deduced what caused it. In general, it is wiser to put more energy into seeing that tantrums are not triggered in the future than into punishing the child for his or her anger. Remember that a tantrum is a response to feelings of helplessness. Allow your child to feel less helpless, and he or she will have less inducement to throw tantrums in the first place.

9. If your child's tantrums don't respond to the above measures, don't lessen with age, or increase in frequency or severity, or if your child becomes dangerous to him/herself or others, or if you simply need

help in understanding, preventing, and controlling tantrums, you should seek professional help.

SEE ALSO

ANGER   BEHAVIOR DISORDERS
FIGHTING   DISCIPLINE

Chapter Eleven
Shyness

"C'mon, Sherry, it's your birthday party! You have to come out. All your friends are here. We can't have the party without you, honey! C'mon, sweetie, come out of your room now. There's nothing to be scared about!"

Sherry is six, and this isn't the first time she's shied away from other people—whether kids her own age, relatives and friends of the family who come for a visit, or strangers she bumps into when she goes out to the mall with her mother. Other people seem to terrify her. Is she socially maladjusted? Is she suffering from some emotional disturbance that will plague her for the rest of her life?

Not necessarily. In fact, a number of studies indicate that as many as 50 percent of all children evince traits associated with shyness. Clearly a good number of normal children react shyly to many social situations. Sometimes shyness is a normal sign of withdrawal at various developmental stages. At seven to nine months, for example, it's normal for an infant to mistrust people who aren't Mommy and Daddy. Similarly, when separation anxiety occurs, at about age two, the child may once again shun unfamiliar people and appear shy. Some children seem constitutionally to have been born shy—it is a fundamental trait of certain personalities, and such children may tend to be quiet throughout much or all of their lives. It's essential to remember that normal temperaments cover a very wide spectrum: The quiet child and the lively, social child may both be quite normal. As always, parents need to sensitize themselves to their children's particular emotional modes of expression and not automatically worry when children don't behave or respond according to some standard that does not apply to them.

There have been many studies of shy children that attempt to sort out what is constitutional and what may be the product of upbringing. Such studies do indicate that the shy child often has at least one shy parent. Shy parents often convey the strong message that novel situations are to be avoided at all costs; caution is the watchword, and the child consequently becomes anxious whenever s/he encounters unfamiliar people or new situations. We do know that there can be an overlap between shyness, anxiety, and social phobia (which are covered in other chapters in this book).

We also know that shyness that may start out as a normal trait can become exacerbated by external influences to become pathological, with a high degree of anxiety, worry, social withdrawal, and other related traits that may persist for a lifetime. These external influences range from such traumas as the illness or death of a parent to child abuse or neglect. Sometimes, ironically, it may be the parents themselves who, in the attempt to get their kids to snap out of it, just worsen the problem. Dealing with a shy child may be especially difficult for a shy parent, who knows from personal experience what the child is feeling and may paradoxically react angrily or critically to the child in the attempt to ameliorate the condition. Unfortunately, this anger and criticism usually accomplish the opposite, making the child even more painfully shy than before.

WHAT TO DO

1. Do not criticize a child for being shy.
2. Before going to a social gathering or other event where the shy child will encounter new people, it is often useful for the parent calmly to outline who will be there and what activities will take place. If possible,

make connections to events the child has gone to and possibly enjoyed before. The parent might rehearse what will happen and what the child might be expected to say or do; rehearsal can very effectively help the child to gain mastery of a new situation.

3. Have the shy child be part of as many small groups and gatherings as possible to give him/her more experience in new social situations. When possible, make sure such groups include one or more adults or children the child knows or with whom s/he feels comfortable.

4. Avoid very large groups whenever possible. Emphasis should be placed on meeting individuals, not on taking on huge numbers of people all at once.

5. Positive reinforcement is particularly effective with shy children. Lavish praise and encouragement on your child whenever s/he succeeds in even the smallest way.

6. Noncompetitive music, arts, or sports clubs and camps are often wonderful experiences for shy children, allowing them to have a sense of mastery and camaraderie without feeling as if they are "less than" if they don't "win."

7. For children for whom the above measures are not helpful, a formal professional desensitization program involving cognitive behavioral techniques may be necessary.

8. For children who do not respond to the measures outlined in suggestions 1 through 6, mild tranquilizers are sometimes prescribed.

It's important to remember that shyness is far more usually a character trait than it is evidence of pathology. It is difficult—and generally wrongheaded—for any of us to try to change character traits, and it is especially demoralizing for children, who simply learn from this kind of coercion that something inside them is "wrong" or "bad" or otherwise unacceptable when really it's just a normal part of who they are. As always, try not to project your own feelings of distress or difficulty onto your child; allow your child to be who s/he really is. Remember that shy people can be just as happy as more extroverted types.

SEE ALSO

ANXIETY	PSYCHOTROPIC MEDICATION
SOCIAL PHOBIA	AND CHILDREN
ALL TYPES OF THERAPY	CHILDREN WHO DON'T SPEAK

CHAPTER TWELVE
Social Phobia

"I was shy when I was a little girl too, Doctor—but nothing like Cheryl. She stays in all weekend—she's terrified she'll run into any other kids outside. And the time she had to read a composition in front of her class—well, that's why I called you. Her teacher said she was so frightened she almost couldn't breathe! What's wrong with her? Have I done anything to cause this?"

Children like Cheryl are often misdiagnosed with many serious syndromes—depression, psychosis, even autism or mutism—when the best overall assessment of their plight is social phobia. Every child suffers some sort of humiliation: insults or nasty nicknames yelled out by a bully in front of other children, feelings of awkwardness, social missteps, painful rejections. But for children who are socially phobic, these inevitable slaps cause them to withdraw from any social contact that presents even the remotest likelihood that they might have to perform in some way and suffer embarrassment.

Sometimes these children become terribly anxious just thinking about the possibility of such a situation, and this anxiety can escalate into a full-fledged panic. As with other phobias, the hallmark of these children's lives becomes avoidance of anyone they feel might judge them to be anxious, weak, incompetent, or in some other way inadequate (all of which they already feel themselves to be). The anxiety socially phobic children feel often manifests physically in a rapid heart rate, stomachaches, sweating, diarrhea, and/or headaches (among many other symptoms). Anticipating a feared social encounter, such children will count the days and the hours with dread, thereby increasing anxiety that was already high to begin with. They will come up with any excuse to avoid the situation. They may literally become sick, somatically manifesting their dread in the relatively minor physical symptoms already mentioned, but sometimes also including more alarming symptoms, such as difficulties in breathing.

Some socially phobic children will explode in anger and tantrums. Most such children cling obsessively to their parents and stay far away from anyone they don't know or trust—which is most of the rest of the world. When meeting anyone new, these children appear overtly anxious, make poor eye contact, and appear inhibited, sometimes to the point of appearing mute. They are timid children, frightened to enter group play, often refusing to go to school. They are extremely sensitive to criticism and rejection and generally have a very low opinion of themselves and their abilities.

The socially phobic child often has appeared shy and timid from birth—which indicates that a tendency toward social phobia may well be inherited. Indeed, most socially phobic children have a parent or other family member who was or still is also socially phobic. Families of socially phobic children do tend to have other anxiety disorders as well. Unfortunately, children who exhibit an early onset of social phobia are more difficult to treat than children in whom the phobia appears later in life. Social phobias do not generally disappear the way many other phobias do. However, with enough support, praise, and reassurance, a socially phobic child does not have to be disabled. Although it is likely such children will always have a tendency to be shy and a bit withdrawn, with help socially phobic children can and do ultimately manage to adjust satisfactorily later in life.

WHAT TO DO

1. Do not minimize or attempt to dismiss your child's social phobia. Take his or her fears and complaints seriously.

2. Don't react to your child's nervousness by becoming nervous yourself, as this will only intensify the problem. Nervousness is contagious.

3. Do not be critical of your child. Socially phobic children have already criticized themselves far more harshly than you would ever think to do. Encouragement, praise, and reassurance are the watchwords here.

4. Do not force your socially phobic child to attend a feared social event prematurely. Rehearse with your child what will happen, and normalize the event as much as possible.

5. Investigate group therapy, particularly with groups of other phobic children, where common fears can be discussed and various feared situations are rehearsed. Children fearful of public speaking might be taken to a tutor sensitive to this phobia. Many professionals run social skills groups that can also be of help. Music and sports lessons can also help to increase a child's feeling of competence and ease his or her social phobia.

6. More intensive psychiatric consultation may be necessary if the social phobia is particularly intransigent. Various medications have proven helpful—specifically mild tranquilizers, some antidepressants, and a group of medications called beta blockers, which, although originally devised to treat heart disease, are also known to calm many of the physical manifestations related to anxiety that afflict socially phobic children.

SEE ALSO

ANXIETY

SCHOOL PHOBIA

PSYCHOTROPIC MEDICATION
  AND CHILDREN

FEARS AND PHOBIAS

ALL TYPES OF THERAPY

CHILDREN WHO DON'T SPEAK

PERVASIVE DEVELOPMENTAL
  DISORDER (AUTISM)

TANTRUMS

ANGER

CHAPTER THIRTEEN

Imaginary Companions

"Arlene sits out at the picnic table talking to some invisible creature she calls Kalamazoo! Is she crazy?"

Children delight in what they conjure up in their play, dreams, and secret thoughts. A child's imagination is powerful and creative enough to invent whole worlds of adventure and possibility—not to mention invisible companions, friends, pets, and other creatures that the child may find very real. In fact, by some measures one-third to half of all children have imaginary companions; even blind children have them. It might be an ideal playmate, a magic fairy godmother, or a big blue talking horse. Some children play host to a horde of different people and animals and elves; others may conjure up only one perfect friend. Parents should not worry when they observe signs of these magical creatures, for more often than not they signal that the child's imagination is in good working order. More frequently evidence of the child's healthy attempt to grapple with internal pressures, hopes, conflicts, dreams, and desires than they are of any chronic or dangerous pathology, these beings are not unlike cherished teddy bears, blankets, dolls, and other toys (what psychologists call transitional objects). They similarly help children to separate from parents and decrease loneliness and feelings of isolation. They also often give young children—usually so exasperatingly subject to adult whims—their first welcome experience of having control over someone or something else. Like an artist, the child who conjures up a personal companion is employing a wonderfully creative medium to externalize and work out many conflicts and behaviors. An invisible friend may be able to get away with bad habits or do "naughty" things the child is not allowed to do—or give expression to thoughts and scenarios that children might be ashamed of or want to keep secret. By projecting "bad" impulses and behavior onto imaginary companions, children are able to vent anxiety and feel more acceptable themselves. This enables the child to differentiate bad from good behavior, become more constructively self-critical, and build a healthy conscience. Imaginary companions especially help the child to deal with inevitable conflicts between individuation and attachment, conflicts with which every human being grapples in different ways from birth to death.

For the most part, imaginary companions are private. They live in a child's room, under the bed, in the closet—although the child sometimes takes them outside as well. (Some have come hand in hand with a little boy or girl into my consultation room.) Most children, when asked, are aware that imaginary companions are not real, and most give them up by the age of six or eight. There is some feeling that they occur more frequently to only children, probably providing them with needed company. Children who are abused or neglected also frequently have imaginary friends, more likely providing some relief to their distress and loneliness than indicating pathology, although in the rare cases where these companions persist beyond the age of nine or ten, frighten the child, or "make" the child act out destructively—all of which seem to occur most often to abused or neglected children— they can be forerunners of deeper trouble, and require professional attention.

WHAT TO DO

1. When parents ask me what to do about their children's imaginary companions, I routinely answer, "Nothing." Allow the child to engage with his or her invisible

friend, remember the healthy adaptation this engagement generally signals, respect the child's privacy, and be assured that the imaginary creature or creatures will almost certainly disappear by the time the child is eight years old.

2. If the child is repetitively misbehaving and blaming his or her imaginary companion for the misbehavior, parents should confront the child with their disbelief and gently but firmly mete out to the child whatever punishment they deem appropriate.

3. Imaginary companions indicate signs of more serious difficulties that require professional consultation only in the following instances:

   a. If the imaginary companion is still present by nine or ten years old.

   b. If the imaginary companion is not usually a warm, friendly, helpful pal but is frightening the child, or if the child believes the companion is making him or her act out in "bad," destructive, or self-destructive ways.

   c. If the imaginary companion seems to take over a child. This usually happens with neglected or abused children and may sometimes be the early forerunner of alternate personalities found in children who have a disorder known as dissociative identity disorder (formerly called multiple personality disorder). However, this is very rare and should not concern the overwhelming majority of parents whose children have imaginary companions.

SEE ALSO

ANXIETY   STRESS

CHAPTER FOURTEEN

Rituals

"Please read that story just one more time. Sit right here on the edge of the bed like before and be sure not to touch my dolls. I want them to sit there just so."

Rituals are behaviors to which many children adhere—such as having the same bedtime story read over and over, lining up bed pillows or stuffed animals in a certain way, only eating certain kinds of food for breakfast or lunch, taking a certain teddy bear everywhere, superstitiously avoiding cracks or lines in the sidewalk ("You'll break your mother's back!")— that often perplex and even embarrass parents.

When my daughter was five, she insisted on wearing the same dress day after day, which meant it had to be washed night after night. Her mother and I were baffled until she finally revealed that she wanted to look like the little girl next door, who wore a uniform to her parochial school, and this dress was the closest thing to that uniform she owned. We were relieved she hadn't just gone off the deep end, but it was still exasperating having to wash that dress!

Rituals are very common and absolutely normal in young children. They supply children with a predictable set of events over which they have some control. This is important for young children, who experience the world as an unpredictable place over which they generally have very little control. These routines, performed ritualistically and repetitively, offer the child a small degree of soothing and calm—even if they can drive parents crazy.

Parents often ask what they should do about these rituals, not only because they sometimes worry that these odd behaviors (and they can appear very strange when you don't know the reason behind them) may be a sign of mental illness, but also because they often interfere with everyday activities and can wreak havoc in the family. They make kids late for school, they interfere with parents' free time at night, they seem to preoccupy children to the point that they may seem socially avoidant, and sometimes they just look so downright odd that the parent is embarrassed by the possibility of anyone outside the family noticing ("They'll think my kid is crazy"). They may be expensive, as when your child may be driven to collect high-cost toys or video games or hard-to-find collectibles. Sometimes the ritualistic behavior disturbs the house by causing noise, isolating the child, interfering with getting up in the morning or going to bed at night, going against what you consider to be correct or polite behavior, or causing unbearable family conflicts with older siblings ("Mommy, make him stop!").

Realizing that rituals are a very common part of early childhood and will more than likely pass as the child matures helps to decrease anxiety. There is no exact timetable for this, but by the time most children enter elementary school, rituals generally have greatly diminished. But don't be surprised if your child's ritual(s) linger a bit longer or reappear at times of stress. See them as inborn behavioral tranquilizers, not unlike many habits adults resort to for self-soothing (jingling coins in the pocket, chewing on a pen, doodling on a scratch pad). However, if they reappear after a relatively long absence, it's a good idea to find out what might be troubling your child and making him or her anxious. It's probably something that, with a little detective work, you can easily discover—and it will not only put your mind at rest, but also help you decide what kind of assistance you might be able to provide your child.

Your child's ritual(s) may be cause for concern if:

- The ritual seriously interferes with any of the regular routines of the day to the point that there is a deterioration in functioning—for example, if the child is unable to dress, get off to school, get to bed in a reasonable amount of time, or interact with other people

- The ritual lasts much longer than expected; for example, if the ritual is still present each day by the age of seven or eight, it's cause for concern

- The child shows signs of severe isolation, social withdrawal, and mild to moderate inability to have normal social relations with other people due to performance of the ritual

- Signs of obsessive-compulsive disorder are present, such as intrusive, anxiety-provoking thoughts or other rigid ritualistic or superstitious behaviors that seem related to your child's attempt to ward off anxiety

- Signs of pervasive developmental disorder (autism) are present, such as severely impaired relations with other people, lack of shared experiences or reciprocity with others, poor speech development, repetitive use of language in a strange way, interest in parts of things but not the whole, and the lack of symbolic play (play that is meaningless and repetitive)

WHAT TO DO

1. If one or both of the first two signs cited above are apparent—your child's ritual is disrupting his/her schedule and family life, and/or the ritual lasts longer than expected—you might try to interfere with the ritual by introducing other activities, limiting the time your child is allowed to indulge in the behavior, or rewarding abstinence with some relished treat or favorite video or other activity. Of course, simply say it's not allowed if the particular ritual might actually harm the child or anyone else (it's obviously taboo if it involves matches, knives, or pulling on the dog's

tail). However, realize that such intervention is always a gamble and must be done with grace. Young children are in the throes of trying to gain control over their world, and telling them too angrily to stop can sometimes just backfire into an unending power struggle. Realize that your child needs to feel some sense of power over his or her environment, and try to suggest alternative activities that will enhance that needed feeling of control.

2. If one or more of the last three warning signs are apparent—significant social problems, signs of obsessive-compulsive disorder, and/or signs of pervasive developmental disorder—you're best advised to seek professional consultation.

SEE ALSO

PERVASIVE DEVELOPMENTAL   ALL TYPES OF THERAPY
DISORDER (AUTISM)   ANXIETY
OBSESSIVE-COMPULSIVE
DISORDER

CHAPTER FIFTEEN

Sleep Disorders

"I can't go to sleep, Mommy! The TV is making too much noise. There's too much light under my door! I'm still thirsty! . . ."

The ability to get a good night's sleep is one of the best and most reliable indications of emotional health for adults as well as children. When a child has trouble sleeping—whether it's insomnia, nightmares, or the relatively rare phenomena of "parasomnias" (sleepwalking and sleep terror disorders)—it usually indicates some deeper underlying anxiety or physical trouble. It also can disrupt the whole household. However, while some sleep disturbances may require special attention, most do not. Over a third of all children experience them at some time of their lives, and most sleep problems tend to go away on their own.

Sleep takes up the major portion of a newborn's life, 60 to 70 percent of the baby's day—even if stretches of an infant's sleep don't always coincide with parental sleeping schedules (think of all those 3 A.M. feedings). Partly this is because the baby is developing internally so rapidly (mentally and physically) that s/he needs to sleep: As serene as a sleeping infant may outwardly appear, an explosion of biological development is going on inside. By the time they are one year old, most babies are able to sleep through the night without waking, especially if they have had a nap or two. Napping decreases as the child grows older (a two-year-old generally only needs one nap during the day). School-age children sleep an average of twelve hours a night.

Children's patterns of sleep can be disturbed by many

things: teething, physical illness, intestinal distress, feeding problems, individual biological temperament, separation anxiety, a loud or chaotic environment, and, later on in childhood, sometimes such conditions as attention deficit disorder, anxiety, and depression. Parents are the best authority when it comes to knowing about a child's sleep patterns and being able to suggest what might be disturbing them. Mothers and fathers have, after all, generally maintained a moment-by-moment connection with their sleeping and waking babies, and nobody knows better than the parent who's had to get up every morning at 3 or 4 A.M. to tend to a crying infant what that baby's normal patterns of sleep tend to be. Parents also know better than anyone else how much the baby may be reacting to separation anxiety—not wanting the parent to go away while the baby is still awake.

The most common sleep disturbance for children is insomnia, defined as the inability, over a period of at least a month, to fall or stay asleep during the night. Insomnia is almost always linked to difficulties the child has with his or her environment. The insomniac child may be overly dependent on his or her parents, nap too much during the day, soak up parental anxiety, have trouble adjusting to different feeding patterns, or experience difficulties in school or with friends and siblings. Sometimes nightmares (which we'll address later on) can be so severe that the child is afraid to go to sleep. However, most children don't need treatment for insomnia, since the condition almost always takes care of itself as the child makes whatever adjustments are necessary. Parents can help by being calm but firm role models, never reacting with too much anxiety to the child's inability to sleep and demonstrating by their own behavior that sleep requires a good amount of time, should be done at regular intervals, and should not be interfered with by such distractions as the television running all night.

Nightmares probably constitute the most frequent sleep disturbance after insomnia. All children have nightmares at some time, and 50 percent have had them regularly at least during some period of early life. Children rarely have nightmares when they first go to sleep; they tend to happen later at night, during REM (rapid eye movement) sleep. Most nightmares involve the fear of physical harm: accidents, being chased, monsters or ghosts. Nightmares usually give expression to conflict over frightening emotions, giving vent to anxiety that the child, as s/he grows and matures, will learn to release in other, less frightening ways during waking hours. After or during a nightmare, children wake up easily and have vivid recall of the dream; they usually are not disoriented or confused, but do feel very frightened and panicky. It may take a good deal of reassurance to get them to go to sleep again, but generally the nightmare will not recur immediately, and the child will be able to sleep peacefully through the rest of the night.

Parasomnias—sleep terrors and sleepwalking—are far less common but much more worrying both to children and parents. In contrast to nightmares, they tend to occur early in the child's sleep, generally in the first three hours of going to bed, during the transition from falling asleep to REM sleep. Sleep terrors (also called night terrors) are well named: The child may suddenly wake up screaming, seem very agitated, and be in danger of running around and hurting him- or herself. Children who suffer from night terrors are disoriented and panicky and unfortunately cannot easily be calmed by parental soothing. However, there is one blessing: Children generally have total amnesia about the incident and when they awaken the next morning rarely remember that it happened.

Sleepwalking similarly takes place early in the sleeping process and the child also rarely remembers having done it. The sleepwalker generally has a blank, staring face and is unresponsive to others who try to communicate with him or her. The best solution is gently to guide the child back to bed and not to wake him or her up during the episode. In contrast to insomnia and nightmares, sleep terrors and sleepwalking generally are not responses to anxiety but seem rather to be reflexive responses—sometimes to psychotropic medication, episodes of fever, or periods of sleeplessness—or possibly the product of inherited susceptibilities. They require more physical than psychological preventive measures: for example, making sure that there are gates at the top of stairs, that there is nothing dangerous on the floor or in the room that the child may bump into, and the like.

WHAT TO DO

1. If your child has insomnia:

    • Make sure that your own anxiety is not contributing to the problem. Remain calm and set a good example yourself of going to sleep and keeping regular habits.

    • Make sure that your home life is not too chaotic, noisy, or likely in other ways to keep your child up.

    • Talk to your child about what might be bothering him or her: Is there a bully in school? Have you recently moved? Is your child having problems with friends or with schoolwork?

    • Reassure your child about any fears you may find irrational. Show him or her that there are no monsters under the bed, that no one will do him/her any harm, and that you are in the house and will keep him/her safe.

    • If the insomnia continues for more than a month, professional help might be important. Family therapy might be indicated, giving you and your child a chance to find out what the child's underlying anxiety is about. Behavioral modification is also very helpful. Medications may sometimes be prescribed on a short-term basis. Hypnosis may also be advisable. A health-care professional will be able to tell if your child suffers from adjustment sleep disorder, which is always related to stressors such as divorce, illness, the death of a loved one, and similar things. It is important to help the child resolve conflicts over these traumas, and such resolution must occur before normal sleep can be resumed.

2. If the child has nightmares:

- Reassure the child that what s/he has just dreamed will not come to pass and that s/he is safe with you in the house. With your child, check closets and under the bed to prove to him or her that there are no monsters to worry about.

- If the nightmares are severe and persistent, professional consultation might be necessary. Therapy concentrates on relieving anxiety, and sometimes the short-term use of medication is recommended.

- Keep in mind that nearly all nightmares have to do with underlying feelings. You know your child's life and history better than any other caregiver; be prepared to fill the therapist in on what you know to aid treatment.

3. If your child suffers from parasomnias (sleepwalking or sleep terrors):

- Do not think of your child as "crazy." Children who suffer from parasomnias rarely suffer from severe emotional problems. Physical safety measures are generally called for, such as locks on doors and windows, gates at the tops of stairs, and so on.

- Do not attempt to awaken your child during a sleepwalking episode; in general, leave the child alone unless he or she seems about to be harmed by or bump into objects in the environment.

- Once you learn what time these episodes generally occur, you might try awakening your child about fifteen minutes beforehand, which may help the child to avoid the episode altogether.

SEE ALSO

SEPARATION ANXIETY   DEPRESSION
ATTENTION DEFICIT DISORDER   ALL TYPES OF THERAPY
ANXIETY   PSYCHOTROPIC MEDICATION
CHILD PHYSICAL ABUSE   AND CHILDREN
SEXUAL ABUSE   STRESS

CHAPTER SIXTEEN
Stealing

"Honest, Mommy, my friend gave it to me! He said he was tired of it. His name? Uh . . . Danny. His last name? Sorry, Mom—he never told me his last name. . . ."

From sandbox "borrowing" and the scream "Finders keepers!" to "I just borrowed it for the night" and "Oh, did I take that? Must have been an accident," the taking of other children's property is virtually universal. In fact, scrap the "virtually": All children do it in the preschool years, and a lot of children continue right through puberty into adolescence. Sometimes what is appropriated turns into a yo-yo from the five-and-ten and later on a pack of cigarettes or even a six-pack of beer from the deli (older kids can be very creative in sneaking off with surprisingly bulky goods, especially on a dare from their peers). This is not news to gladden a parent's heart, maybe, but it's also rarely a sign of major trouble—another fairly typical misbehavior in which nearly every kid occasionally indulges.

In fact, the very young child—before about three—doesn't know the difference between him/herself and others, and certainly can't differentiate whose possessions are whose. You could hardly call anything the typical two-year-old does "stealing." As toddlerhood continues and preschool approaches, a sense begins to develop of "me" versus "not me," "yours" versus "mine"—and stealing begins to have meaning.

What does stealing signify once it has meaning for the child? Different things, possibly, at different times. Done by especially young children, stealing usually represents an effort to make up for some need not being filled by the parents for more involvement in the family or simply for more attention. Such stealing is not serious and actually can serve as a sign to the parent that the child wants and needs more involvement—it can offer the opportunity to establish a stronger and warmer bond with your child. Even later on in childhood, stealing usually signals that the child needs and wants more attention, perhaps due to parental preoccupation with other issues or siblings, physical illness, or another child being ill. The child perceives a threat to his/her feeling of being loved and cared for by his/her parents. That's why it's especially common to see episodes of stealing at times of family stress such as divorce or separation, a parent's loss of a job, or moving. These episodes of stealing usually pass rather quickly as the child adjusts to the new situation or contact between child and parents is reestablished.

Stealing is serious and indicates more long-standing psychological issues when it:

- Is persistent
- Is associated with other phenomena such as aggression against others (people or animals), destruction of property, deceitfulness, and serious violation of rules—all symptoms of behavior disorders
- Is remorseless
- Is clearly hostile
- Is associated with egocentrism and poor interpersonal relations
- Gets the attention of authorities such as police and/or teachers
- Is not understandable or responsive to intervention
- Seems out of control

Stealing associated with the above characteristics indicates a serious problem in the development of the particular child with and in his/her family. There are often severe family stresses, some degree of emotional deprivation, poor parental role modeling, and often covert encouragement of such behaviors. A child who persistently steals often also has an underlying depression or anxiety condition and a high propensity to express rage and hostility toward adults.

WHAT TO DO

Although most stealing isn't serious, parents shouldn't condone stealing (even if they can remember doing it themselves as kids) or welcome it as a communicative behavior. The following steps should be taken:

1. See the stealing as the expression of a child's need to restore a solid bond with his/her parents and try to correct whatever has gone wrong or broken this essential contact. Of course, a divorce or other permanent strain cannot be changed, but recognizing and discussing the feelings of the child and assuming a curious and receptive stance toward him/her can go a long way to ameliorating disturbing feelings and stop the symptoms of stealing.

2. Check to see if you haven't been pressuring your child in some way that wasn't so apparent (at least to you).

3. Find out if your child's friends are exerting peer pressure on him/her to steal.

4. Always set limits and let a child know that even if you understand what the stealing is about, it is not acceptable. Taking other people's property will not be permitted, and the stolen property must be returned or paid for by the child with or without your assistance.

5. If the stealing recurs, then appropriate punishments should be instituted, such as working to make money to pay for the object stolen (if it cannot be returned),

age-appropriate early curfews or no weekends away from home, limited playtime after school, and so on. Make sure your child knows why he/she is being punished, reinforcing the message that stealing is undesirable and that the stolen property must be returned.

In the overwhelming majority of cases of childhood stealing, such measures will help a child, and the stealing will be seen as a transient reaction to stress or a means of communicating parent-child problems that can be resolved with increased awareness and attention.

When stealing is serious, professional help is required because the stealing has become part of a more complex and deep-seated disturbance, such as a behavior disorder, depression, or a long-standing parent-child problem that the parent and child cannot resolve themselves.

Appropriate psychotherapy may involve one or more of the following:

- Individual therapy
- Family therapy
- Special group therapy for behavior disorders
- Possibly special residential treatment

SEE ALSO

BEHAVIOR DISORDERS	ANGER
DEPRESSION AND MANIA	ANXIETY
STRESS	ALL TYPES OF THERAPY

CHAPTER SEVENTEEN

Lying

"Where's my beach ball? A—a big seagull took it, Mommy! He came flying down out of the sky and he was as big as— as—an airplane! He chased me all the way down the beach!"

Billy's story about the airplane-sized seagull taking his beach ball does not indicate he's having a psychotic breakdown. Billy is five. You could call his story a tall tale or more bluntly a lie, but in fact he's doing what many children his age do: letting his imagination rule and create a more palatable and interesting reality. Actually, Billy doesn't know what happened to his beach ball, and he probably suspects he'll be in a fix if he doesn't come up with some reason why he lost it. So he resorts to his storytelling resources to help him out of it. He's not really lying—he half believes a huge bird did fly out of the sky and rob him of his toy!

Until they are six or seven years old, most children do not know the difference between wishful thinking, imagination, and what is real. Imaginary thinking, imaginary playmates, and vivid fantasies remain quite meaningful parts of the small child's life. This is why expecting a child under seven years old to tell the truth is inappropriate. However, after the age of seven we can increasingly expect children to know the difference between the truth and a lie. So why do children this age and older lie? The same reasons anyone lies who is conscious of it: to cover up actions they know will bring on displeasure and disapproval, or to boost their self-image by showing off and "improving" what they believe are the far too modest facts about themselves. Sometimes these exhibitionist liars do start to believe the self-aggrandizing tales they tell about themselves—largely because their self-esteem is so low that they desperately want to believe them.

Parents should not be alarmed by lies their small children tell. It becomes a matter for concern only if the lying is compulsive or widespread, and especially if it is associated with other antisocial acts such as those found in children with a behavior disorder. Deceitfulness is a common core symptom of children who have serious behavior disorders but is usually seen along with other aggressive and hostile behaviors—violations of rules, stealing, substance abuse, and other delinquent acts.

WHAT TO DO

1. If your child is younger than seven years old and lies, do not chastise, punish, spank, or in any other way humiliate him or her for the mistruth. Remember that most young children grow to have a normal sense of morality and conscience and that "fantastic" lying will decrease in time.

2. As your child develops the ability to tell the truth, he or she should be praised, particularly if it was hard to be truthful (e.g., admitting doing something wrong). Positive reinforcement of the child's good behavior goes a lot further than punishing him or her for telling a lie.

3. For children older than seven who lie to cover up accidents or deliberately disobedient acts in order to avoid punishment, make it clear that while telling a lie might work in the short run, eventually it will diminish the child's credibility. Reassure your child that reasonable punishment for an infraction doesn't mean you don't love the child. Make it clear that he or she will feel much better if the habit of telling the truth is adopted. The story of the boy who cried wolf is a useful parable here.

4. Be a good role model for your child: Make sure you don't lie. This isn't always as easy as it may seem, particularly when your child hears you telling white lies that may be designed to save someone's feelings or bolster their self-esteem (e.g., "Oh, I think you look great in that dress!" or "It's really delicious—I'm just so full I can't eat another bite"). This is confusing to a child, who tends to take a much more black-and-white view of things. Try not to tell white lies in front of very young children; with older children, explain the difference.

5. Professional help is indicated if, as noted above, your child's lying is compulsive and accompanies other aggressive and antisocial acts. Lying is then part of a larger pathological picture, and your child should be seen by a mental health-care professional.

SEE ALSO

BEHAVIOR DISORDERS   ALL TYPES OF THERAPY

CHAPTER EIGHTEEN
Fire Setting

"I don't know what's gotten into Bart. Yesterday I found him throwing lit matches into the trash can! I had to put the fire out with the garden hose. And just now I got a call from his third-grade teacher. She says Bart and some other kids keep lighting fires on the school playground. I punish him and tell him how dangerous it is, but he just shuts down and gets sullen. Why does he keep doing this?"

Bart is eight years old—which is the average age of the child who repetitively lights fires for the thrill of it and/or with malicious intent. Fire setting is a serious problem. It's one of the major causes of death in preschoolers and the second most frequent cause of death in children six to fourteen years old. Sixty percent of children engage in some type of innocent fire play—it usually proceeds from a natural curiosity about fire that most children have from about the age of three. The majority of these children do it only once, and the fires they set are accidental. If the fire gets out of control, they do all they can to put it out. They are not fire setters. Bart, however, may be.

True fire setting is characterized by its deliberateness and the frequency with which it is carried out. Younger children typically set fires at home, but fire setters tend to set them away from home—often at school. Often a teacher is the target of the fire setting, with the motive often revenge. The fire setter also does it for the excitement, and frequently does it with a group of other children. Instead of trying to put out the fire, fire setters run away, stay out of sight, and may watch the fire engines pull up to put the fire out.

Fire setting is rarely an isolated symptom in such children. Fire setters often come from families in which there has been divorce, a recent death, or other problems that lead to lack of supervision, chaos, and neglect. Most children who engage in fire setting have normal intelligence, but they tend to display a higher degree of attention deficit disorder and learning disabilities. They're usually angry children who have shown aggressive behaviors in many other areas of life. They're often impulsive and hyperactive and have frequent episodes of rage. For children who feel especially powerless, setting fires seems to give them a yearned-for rush of feeling powerful. Often such children have been sexually abused or physically punished. They may come from families exhibiting a high degree of psychopathology, frequently involving substance abuse. They generally have poor relationships with other children and are known by school authorities as troubled and troubling children. The typical fire setter often suffers from the psychiatric syndrome known as conduct disorder; a small percentage of fire setters suffer from schizophrenia or other psychotic disorders, or sometimes organic brain disease. There is an increased incidence of fire setting in mentally retarded children, probably due to their lack of awareness of its dangers. In younger children who light fires there seems to be an association with various signs of immaturity such as thumb sucking, bed-wetting, and stuttering.

We don't know all the reasons why fire setting is displayed as a symptom by some children and not others. There have been many theories about its causes, including Freud's insistence that it has to do with conflicts involving sexual instincts, as well as various suggested connections to learning, socialization, and family pathology.

WHAT TO DO

1. Parents should teach their children about the dangers of fire when they are young, and continue to teach them as they grow older and become more capable of setting fires themselves—including pointing out how

gas stoves, charcoal grills, matches, fireplaces, and other such things work.

2. Never underestimate the curiosity your children have about fire and their propensity to be fascinated and seduced by it.

3. Fire play should not be tolerated at all, and flammable materials should be kept away from children.

4. Take your child to the local fire department. You will usually find cooperative fire personnel who have developed many different effective strategies for teaching children and parents about how to avoid fires at home.

5. If fire play continues and you believe your child has more than a transient age-appropriate curiosity about fire, consider that the problem is significant and requires professional attention. It is probable that your child is angry and defiant and exhibits other symptoms and traits covered in the foregoing overview; it is also probable that your family relations and home life are strained and need attention.

6. Many programs are available to help children who are fire setters, which generally is only one of a number of symptoms that indicate a larger disorder. Therapeutic interventions include individual, family, and behavioral therapy, and sometimes institutional or residential placement for the more severe cases.

SEE ALSO

BEHAVIOR DISORDERS   ALL TYPES OF THERAPY
ANGER   SCHIZOPHRENIA
ENURESIS (WETTING)   SEXUAL ABUSE
STEALING   CHILD PHYSICAL ABUSE
ATTENTION DEFICIT   LEARNING DISORDERS
  DISORDER   STRESS

Chapter Nineteen
The Bully and the Bullied

"When Caitlin's teacher called and said they were having problems with a classroom bully, I flashed on how scared I'd been of a nasty bruiser who had threatened me back in third grade. 'Is Caitlin hurt?' I asked. 'No,' the teacher said. 'But the little boy she beat up in the playground isn't doing too well.' I couldn't believe it—Caitlin was the bully."

Despite the welcome fact that by the time they reach the third or fourth grade most children no longer resort to fighting as their primary means of settling disputes, some children seem to stay stuck in the bullying mode. Who doesn't remember a bully from the neighborhood or the playground—that bigger, tougher kid who intimidated everybody, whom you'd walk blocks and blocks out of the way to avoid, who maybe even entered your nightmares? Or maybe *you* were the kid the other kids stayed clear of. (How many of us actually remember being the bully?) Bullying—the use of force and intimidation as coercion—is, unfortunately, a common enough tactic within the family, among parents and siblings. But it's also a very common source of trouble—sometimes not insignificant trouble—outside the home as well: in the neighborhood, at school, at camp, at the beach, on the playground.

Usually perpetrated by an older and/or tougher child on a younger, weaker, or more passive child, bullying tends to rob the victim not only of self-esteem but sometimes of money and possessions as well. Bullying can involve more serious cases of assault and sexual submission. At a time when children seem to have greater access to firearms and other lethal weapons than ever before, bullying can even turn into murder. (Not all bullies are the pretenders common wisdom would like us to think they are.)

Like Caitlin's mother, our sympathies tend to run first to the victims of bullies. However, the bully—the victimizer—is often far more badly impaired than the child who is victimized by the bully. A young child described as a fearless show-off always looking for victims to dominate often becomes the adolescent with a full-fledged conduct disorder and the adult criminal whose life is spent in and out of prison. Bullies tend to learn bullying at home. They often were and are disciplined by being hit. Aggressive parenting creates a hostile home atmosphere, often added to by frequent episodes of domestic violence between parents and/or among parents and siblings. Witnessing all this not only reinforces the lesson that violence and intimidation are effective coping tactics, but tends to deaden any concern with the feelings of others. This is made vivid to me when I first do a one-on-one interview with a child accused of bullying and then meet the child's parents, who often bully me during the family discussion. The sad fact is that despite his (or *her*—Caitlin reminds us that bullying among girls is getting more common, although the great majority of bullies are still boys) outward bravado and arrogance, the bully is typically anxious, depressed, angry, and hurt—feelings often passed down wholesale from the bully's parents. Worse, the bullying child is not generally amenable to talking about feelings or trying to understand his or her own behavior. Bullies resolve angry feelings by identifying with them and getting angry at others.

Not that victims of bullies don't suffer sometimes significant damage from their victimization. Bullies typically pick their victims very cannily: The children they harass are often nervous, worried, anxious, insecure—in some ways displaying exactly the same feelings the bully has repressed. Children who are frequently bullied often become paralyzed and can't fight back. Thus they tend to become the victims of repetitive bullying, over time developing the reputation of being "easy marks," easily intimidated by any new bully who comes along looking for fresh prey. They frequently haven't learned to assert themselves appropriately, and the bully in the neighborhood—with an uncanny radar—can often sense who they are. They may not tell their parents because of the humiliation they suffer, but may develop somatic symptoms or school phobia in order to avoid the pain of being picked on.

The bully and the bullied are cousins under the skin. Each deals with crippling insecurity and feelings of helplessness in the face of anger: in the bully's case, the anger s/he sees at home and can resolve only by identifying with it and acting it out; in the bullied child's case, the anger s/he feels internally and feels s/he must take out on him/herself. While probably no child entirely escapes some experience of bullying or being bullied and the net effects don't generally have a lasting debilitating effect, bullying can become a serious problem when:

1. Your child has become a bully to the point of causing physical harm and disruption

2. The school or other outside observers report such behavior in your child

3. Bullying is associated with other disturbing and angry behaviors such as those found in children with behavior disorder

4. Your child becomes a victim, fears humiliation, and becomes passive, depressed, overtly insecure, nervous, and avoidant

WHAT TO DO IF YOUR CHILD IS A BULLY

1. You must first be sure that you are not providing a model for his or her behavior. This is always one of

the most difficult parts of being a good parent: examining our own behavior for the example it may be providing our children. Corporal punishment has no place in a healthy family. It teaches the child one lesson: that you can get what you want through physical force.

2. If your child can't stop being a bully—if s/he compulsively or repetitively bullies other children—s/he needs professional help. You may want to start with the school's guidance counselor, and/or then pursue a mental health-care professional. The quicker bullying is addressed the better; if it is not, it can set up a dangerous pattern for your child that may result in far more serious and disruptive conduct disorders later on.

WHAT TO DO IF YOUR CHILD IS THE VICTIM OF A BULLY

1. Help him or her to talk about it—establish an atmosphere conducive to talking about the feelings of shame and humiliation s/he may feel. Don't leap in with suggestions or quick judgments; such attempts to help are often experienced by the child as a kind of psychic bullying. For the most part, you should encourage your child to speak directly with the authority figure responsible for harmony and safety (teacher, principal, swimming pool director, etc.) to give your child an active, assertive role in resolving the problem. Rushing in to fix it for your child (i.e., by contacting the bullying child's parents and demanding an apology) may ultimately worsen the problem; at the very least, you and your child should work together to deal with the bully. Your child should have some experience of "fighting back" so

that s/he does not simply feel further victimized. It helps to have your child understand the psychology of the bully, that s/he simply is egged on by overly passive or insecure behaviors and that some amount of confident and even humorous self-assertion can often help your child to get through the next ominous encounter. However, don't encourage your child to fight physically, which will just escalate the violence (possibly with significant danger to your child) and reinforce fighting as a solution. Even very young children can understand that "something's wrong with" or "bothering" a bully; let your child know that, deep down, the bully is an unhappy creature and that his/her unhappiness really has nothing to do with your child.

2. If your child cannot overcome his or her fear and anxiety about a bully, it is wise to seek outside help, especially if fear, anxiety, and depression are interfering with day-to-day life. Support your child's friendships and social network throughout the ordeal of dealing with a bully; this is the time when your child most needs to feel s/he is not ostracized because of being the bully's victim.

SEE ALSO

FIGHTING   ANGER
SCHOOL PHOBIA   PSYCHOSOMATIC DISORDERS
ANXIETY   ALL TYPES OF THERAPY

CHAPTER TWENTY
Fighting

"Mommy! Jenny just smacked me on the head again with my Barbie doll!"

Six-year-old Margaret is complaining about her two-year-old sister, Jenny. Isn't Jenny a bit young to be fighting? If you have a two-year-old, you know she isn't. In fact, Jenny started "fighting" when she was eighteen months old. This doesn't mean that she's abnormally aggressive. All children fight. In fact, fighting is such a ubiquitous practice with children that it only rarely appears in psychiatric literature as a separate phenomenon; we take it for granted that from time to time children will get into scuffles and make their anger known in a push, slap, bite, scratch, or bop over the head with a Barbie doll.

Fighting between toddlers typically erupts over attempts to "share" toys or other belongings. Sharing is a foreign concept to very young children, who can become especially possessive of what they perceive belongs to them. They often see nothing wrong in appropriating another toddler's toy; in fact, they'll fight to get it and fight to keep it. Later on, passing through various stages of separation anxiety and normal apprehensiveness about other children in the neighborhood, on the playground, or in the classroom, school-age children also typically vent their anger and frustration in fighting. We do expect that by the second or third grade, children no longer automatically resort to physical fights to settle disputes. From this age children can be persuaded to talk through disagreements rather than hit or kick or throw something at each other to make their points.

Although fighting is normal to some degree, there are certain conditions that make fighting more common in particular children. These almost always have to do with less-than-optimal family dynamics. When home life is chaotic and disruptive, and especially when physical aggression is used in a family to win arguments, children have role models teaching them that fighting is an acceptable coping tactic, and they can be expected to fight in and out of the home. Children who are spanked fight more, children who need attention fight more, and children who see all around them that most issues are settled through violence, intimidation, and verbal abuse fight more. Often children who have been sexually abused fight more. Children who have been shamed, humiliated, dominated, or otherwise handled in a way that makes them feel powerless also tend to fight more. In other words, family structure and the subculture in which a child lives often indicate which children will fight more than others. There is also the effect of the larger culture and media—particularly television and movies—in which violence is so rampant and seemingly unimportant that children have become desensitized to it. This can lead to more fighting too.

Fighting is a problem that may require attention or intervention if:

1. It is compulsive and repetitive and appears to be the only way your child knows how to express his/her feelings of distress and anger.
2. It becomes widespread, so that it affects school performance and social adjustment.
3. Your child has become a bully or a victim of one repetitively.
4. It involves getting in trouble with the police or other authorities.
5. It is associated with other problems indicating a more widespread disorder, such as fire setting, stealing, van-

dalism, and compulsive lying, or if it is associated with symptoms of attention deficit disorder such as inattention, hyperactivity, and impulsivity.

6. It is associated with neurological problems.

7. It is associated with learning disorders.

8. Your child's fighting becomes part of being socialized into a gang. Gang violence is more serious than non-gang violence because it more often results in lethal assaults and weapons used against other gangs.

WHAT TO DO

1. First of all, understand that occasional fighting is no cause for alarm. It is, however, your job as a parent to make sure that neither your child nor any child s/he may be fighting is unduly physically harmed. It's also never too early to encourage your child to settle disputes verbally and to vent his or her feelings of distress to you freely so that they don't back up—and end up acted out in a fight.

2. As always, the model you provide for your children is the best teacher. If you resort to fighting or violence in the home, the likelihood is that your child will do so too.

3. Limit your child's exposure to gratuitous violence in movies and video games, on television, and on the Internet.

4. Professional help is needed when any of the conditions in the above list ("Fighting is a problem . . . if ") prevail.

5. Fighting as a separate symptom, when it is perceived to be a problem requiring treatment, is generally dealt with by one form or another of behavioral therapeutic intervention. However, family therapy, individual

psychotherapy, and sometimes group therapy will be necessary to deal with the larger issues, of which fighting is only a part. Some children's aggression may be so out of control that psychopharmacological intervention is necessary. Various medications including clonidine, antipsychotics, and even antidepressants have been used in children who display unusual degrees of aggressiveness.

SEE ALSO

BEHAVIOR DISORDERS

CHILD PHYSICAL ABUSE

SEXUAL ABUSE

ANGER

THE BULLY AND THE BULLIED

FIRE SETTING

STEALING

LYING

ATTENTION DEFICIT DISORDER

LEARNING DISORDERS

ALL TYPES OF THERAPY

PSYCHOTROPIC MEDICATION
   AND CHILDREN

MEDIA AND CHILDREN

DISCIPLINE

Chapter Twenty-one
Behavior Disorders

"I don't know what to do, Doctor! Jimmy talks when he's not supposed to in class, throws paper airplanes, pushes kids around at school recess, keeps getting into fights. The teacher keeps punishing him—I keep punishing him—and he looks at us like we're crazy! He honestly doesn't seem to know that what he's doing is wrong!"

Jimmy's parents are typical of fully half of the parents who come to see me: Their children have what they or their teacher call "behavioral problems." In one way or another, they're not behaving according to the standards of their families, schools, churches, or the rules posted in the public park where they're playing: They're "misbehaving," or being "bad." Like Jimmy, most children who misbehave don't believe they have a problem—what they're doing seems perfectly natural and right to them. They may be genuinely confused when they're told they're doing the wrong thing. This brings up perhaps the most important thing to remember about children's misbehavior: The people the child affects are more likely to see the child as a problem than the child him- or herself.

Children aren't born possessing values, manners, codes of ethics, or standards of behavior. They learn them from outside influences—parents, teachers, older siblings, friends, movies, television, and the Internet. Parents are often baffled that their children don't somehow automatically know what's right and wrong, not realizing that a child must always determine for him- or herself what is right and wrong from the lessons s/he is taught and from the example of people around him or her. These lessons and examples may be teaching the child quite different moral values than the parents believe, wish, or hope the child is getting. Additionally, behavior is also influenced by temperament; as you've seen in so many other discussions in this book, each child is uniquely the product of his or her own genetic legacy and family and cultural influences. There are quiet children who seem naturally to behave politely and follow the rules they're given; there are noisy and rambunctious kids who can't seem to stay in their skins and tend to be the ones who throw softballs through the picture window. But neither child is abnormal—they just have different styles of behavior.

Unfortunately, our own temperaments as parents inevitably color our first reactions to what we may judge to be the misbehavior of our children, whose inborn temperaments can differ quite widely from our own. Picture the sports-minded dad who sees his little boy "misbehaving" because he's not participating in Little League or otherwise showing an aggressive interest in sports, or the mild and meek mother who thinks her daughter is "misbehaving" because she is loud and boisterous and always wants to be first in line. These are obvious examples of the traps parents can and do fall into as they apply their own expectations and standards of behavior to their children without regard for who their children really are temperamentally.

Indeed, there is no area in child psychiatry that relies more on the evaluation of the parent than the realm of children's behavior problems. With very few exceptions—attention deficit disorder primary among them—behavior problems in children are learned. The source of distress is nearly always either the parents' own reactions to their children's behavior and temperaments or the examples the parents wittingly or unwittingly set. This suggests very strongly that if you've got a child who "misbehaves," you are well advised first to sort out your own childhood legacies and worries and expectations (which often manifest as being overly concerned with what

other people will think) from the needs and temperament of
your child. Learn to see your child for who she or he really
is, and you'll have come a long way toward being able to deal
with, by better understanding the sources of, your child's
"misbehavior." Not that that softball through the picture
window should go unpunished, but it shouldn't automatically be seen as pathological behavior.

Examining your own assumptions probably will reveal
which of two common biases you tend to hold: (1) that your
child behaves as s/he does because of inborn reflexes and
temperament, or (2) that your child's behavior is simply the
result of how s/he happens to be feeling at the moment. The
parent who subscribes to the first belief will generally construct a framework for the child of rewards, punishments,
rules, and discipline on the assumption that reflexes must be
brought into line. The parent who subscribes to the second
belief tends to be softer and more flexible, seeking to understand the child's feeling state rather than to imposing strict
rules for behavior. You can see that each pole has its dangers:
the first, that the child's feelings may be neglected or dis-
missed; the second, that the child will be given too free a
rein and not be subject to necessary boundaries. Clearly we
are all combinations of temperament and emotional influences; parents need to see their children from both stand-
points, and respond to their children with a view to what the
child needs at that particular moment.

Behavior is diagnosed by mental health-care professionals
as a problem largely according to its chronic disruptiveness. Most children misbehave now and then—according to
temperament, some may throw a lot more softballs through
windows than others—and whatever the degree of occasional misbehavior, more than likely these children will not
turn into pathologically aggressive or destructive adults. The
problem comes when disruptiveness is persistent. Indeed,
the psychiatric terms for child misbehavior that requires
attention derive essentially from their persistently disruptive

character. They are attention deficit disorder (dealt with elsewhere in this book), oppositional defiant disorder, and conduct disorder. We diagnose a conduct disorder when the child chronically and repetitively violates rules, disregards societal norms appropriate to his or her age, and/or violates the basic rights of individuals or destroys the environment. Oppositional defiant disorder is characterized by a persistent lack of cooperation, hostility, and defiance to authority and may include temper tantrums, arguing, breaking rules, refusing requests, and annoying other people. This behavior may occur at home, at school, in the neighborhood, or all three. These children often blame others for their problems, show very little insight, and seem always to be angry—prone at any moment to attack others, destroy property, and use foul language. Anger may especially flare up over issues such as eating, sleeping, toilet training, and other circumstances or situations in which a parent attempts to lay down the law. In other words, oppositional and defiant children seem to be exaggerated examples of the toddler stage commonly referred to as the "terrible twos"—that time in early childhood when oppositional defiance is a quite normal expression of adaptation to a new developmental stage, a sign that the child is striving to separate from the parent and assert more independence. The older oppositional defiant child is, however, stuck in defiance and does not move through it as a stage. Typically such children suffer from depression due to rejection by peers, families, and teachers.

Let me say here, once and for all, that there is no such thing as a bad seed. As widely as our temperaments may vary, no child is born with a conduct or oppositional defiant disorder. There is no proven genetic alteration that makes children constitutionally disordered or pathologically disruptive and aggressive. This is not to say that we know definitively what the biological origins of temperament are, or that there may not be certain inborn susceptibilities to impatience, anger, and rambunctiousness. Indeed, we do tend to see certain common emotional states in children with conduct and oppositional defiant disorders: suspiciousness, depression, irritability, anger, impulsivity, and an intolerance for frustration. These emotional states may most often be the product of negative environmental conditioning, as these children often come from homes in which there is family instability and disorganization or where the parents themselves may be mentally ill.

While some studies have attempted to link brain abnormalities and low levels of serotonin, norepinephrine, or dopamine to these disorders, by far the greatest cause of these disorders appears to be negative environmental influences. Children exhibiting conduct and oppositional defiant disorders typically have been exposed to violence and parental mental or emotional problems. They were often abused. They also often come from homes where there is parental deprivation, housing difficulties, too little food and comfort, and sometimes medical problems that long go undiagnosed. When deprivation is severe enough, some children diagnosed with these disorders may actually become psychotic and lose touch with shared reality. As the result of severe abuse, some children suffer from dissociative identity disorder or post-traumatic stress disorder. At very young ages they may become dependent on alcohol or abuse drugs. It's unsurprising that many such children also suffer from learning disabilities, attention deficit disorder, retardation, or seizures.

Fortunately, conduct and oppositional defiant disorders are quite rare. The important point for most parents is to try to understand the natural temperaments of their children as distinct from their own expectations, first of all to determine what is normal behavior for each child so that the child's "misbehavior" can be better understood. Remember that the watchwords in diagnosing the more serious disorders are persistence and repetitiveness. The categories of chronic misbehavior that appropriately cause concern and require professional treatment are these:

1. Aggression against people and animals (torturing pets or wild animals or insects, hitting or hurting another child or person, etc.)

2. Destruction of property (fire setting, smashing glass, throwing toys out windows or down stairs, etc.)

3. Deceitfulness and theft (breaking into people's houses or cars, stealing from a victim on the street, shoplifting, etc.)

4. Serious violations of rules (persistently breaking parental curfews, running away, truancy from school, etc.)

WHAT TO DO

1. The first thing to keep in mind is that most children with occasional disruptive behaviors do not go on to become antisocial, violent, abusive, or criminal adults. Defiant behavior is often a normal part of growing up, and will pass on its own.

2. Try to see what the underlying cause of the misbehavior is—whether it is being triggered by issues that even the child may not be aware of. Does the child misbehave more at school than at home? Does it happen more often at a particular time of day? Do certain people bring out the worst in your child—including parents and family members? Does it happen right before moments of stress—the first day of school, vacation, before traveling? Parents are often the best diagnosticians of what the real impetus is for misbehavior, and thus the best people to help the child deal with the real problem. Remember that young children especially may not be able to express their distress except by acting out. You can help them to express it by attempting to empathize with what the problem really is.

3. The best ways to cure your child of misbehaving is

to give him or her a positive example. Keep a lid on your own irrational or angry outbursts. Offer positive reinforcement, constructive criticism, and compassionate attention to your child. Let your child see you deal with stress and difficulty without undue anxiety. These are the lessons that will hit home, not whatever you may put into a lecture.

4. If anger becomes extremely disruptive, use anger first aid (described in Chapter 3).

5. If you can't identify the trigger for your child's misbehavior and/or your attempts to empathize and guide the child don't work, you may need to seek professional help. Sometimes doing this even once or twice can help; an objective observer can help you and your child to see issues more clearly.

6. If a few sessions with a professional don't help, then have your child tested by a professional competent in the fields of learning disabilities, organic brain disease, psychosis, depression, attention deficit disorder, and dissociative identity disorder.

7. Treatment of a child with a behavior disorder is usually multimodal—that is, it involves the child and his/her family and takes place not only in the professional's office but back at home as well as in schools or community centers. Parents are often taught different ways to interact with the child, to break the repetitive cycles of negative reinforcement. This is done through family therapy, lectures, and in groups involving other families with such children who meet to vent, share, and find support. The child can also participate in individual psychotherapy or learn social skills and problem solving from a professional skilled in those areas. The point is that therapy for such children can't be limited to once a week; the whole family needs to work with the child in and out of a professional's of-

fice. If the disorder is particularly acute or severe, sometimes a child will need medication such as psychotropic drugs.

SEE ALSO

ATTENTION DEFICIT DISORDER

DEPRESSION AND MANIA

ANGER

SEXUAL ABUSE

CHILD PHYSICAL ABUSE

FIGHTING

FIRE SETTING

LEARNING DISORDERS

DOES MY CHILD NEED TESTING?

ALL TYPES OF THERAPY

PSYCHOTROPIC MEDICATION
   AND CHILDREN

DISCIPLINE

Chapter Twenty-two
Attention Deficit
Disorder

"Jimmy, if I have to tell you to stay in your seat one more time . . ."

As a child matures, he or she develops patience and the ability to focus on a topic or activity for longer and longer periods of time. Some children have developed the ability to sit, listen, and follow most commands by the time they enter preschool; many others achieve this by the time they enter kindergarten, and nearly all children do by the time they reach the second or third grade. That's not to say that there isn't great variability within any group of children. Each child has his or her own unique timetable and course of development. Children differ widely in activity levels (this is noticeable even at birth) as well as in their capacity to be patient and their ability to focus, remember, and organize themselves around certain tasks. Walk into a nursery and already you'll see a wide spectrum of activity levels; visit a preschool or even a kindergarten and you'll similarly see a host of different developmental styles and levels of mastery, from the quiet, absorbed little girl in the corner who is careful to keep her crayoning within the outlines of her coloring book to the lively, easily distracted boy who cracks jokes and flies his paper airplane over her head. In fact, there's no child who fits every textbook aspect of "normal" development: Every child is an individual, developing in his or her own time and way.

But for some children, inattention, hyperactivity, and/or

impulsivity remain past second or third grade and may even intensify as the child grows older. These children sometimes suffer from attention deficit disorder (ADD, also called attention deficit hyperactivity disorder, or ADHD), a diagnosis that has received so much attention in the media that many parents are fearful that a child showing any liveliness or impatience whatsoever might be afflicted with the disorder. At the other extreme, some people claim that there's no such thing as ADD, that doctors and drug companies routinely misdiagnose as pathological children who aren't abnormal at all but are simply a bit more active, a little less patient, and perhaps a little less gifted than others.

All any of these skeptics has to do is spend one day with a child with ADD to be convinced beyond doubt that the syndrome exists. Children with ADD perpetually get into trouble; teachers complain that their ability to concentrate is markedly less than others'. They are poorly organized, have short attention spans, chronically forget and/or lose their belongings, seem incapable of listening or following directions, and become distracted by the slightest disturbance. At home, starting in earliest toddlerhood for some, these children always seem to be on the go: running, climbing, tripping, motor-mouthing, getting into everything, and just being downright hard to control or contain. They can't wait long for anything and tend to be intensely competitive—even pushy or bossy.

It is true that ADD afflicts a minority of children and is sometimes misdiagnosed. Reliable estimates indicate that up to about 7 percent of all school-age children suffer from this disorder. Not everyone exhibits all of the symptoms. Some children may be inattentive; others may be hyperactive as well. Nearly all tend to be impulsive. While it used to be thought that boys suffered from ADD more than girls, recent findings seem to imply that more ADD boys have the hyperactive component and thus tend to be more disruptive than girls, leading to the erroneous conclusion that more boys have the ADD syndrome.

Unfortunately, many children with ADD also suffer from other behavioral disturbances, problems with mood and self-image, anxiety, depression, and feelings of exclusion, rejection, and isolation. Close to half of all children with ADD have learning disabilities as well, such as dyslexia (inability to read well), dyscalculia (inability to do mathematics well), and dysgraphia (inability to write well). We now know that ADD can be a lifelong disorder that if not treated in childhood often leads to many negative consequences in later years. Teenagers and adults who had ADD in childhood not only are sometimes plagued by the same residual problems they suffered as kids (inattention, impulsivity, hyperactivity), but also are more likely to commit antisocial acts, abuse alcohol and drugs, have more car accidents, suffer from poor self-esteem, and on the whole accomplish less than their unafflicted peers. These are important reasons why early diagnosis and treatment are essential.

No one is sure what causes this syndrome. There seems to be some evidence for genetic transmission of ADD, but there is as much evidence that environmental stress, such as bonding difficulties and family and/or parenting problems, also plays a key role. There is no conclusive evidence that diet, specific brain abnormalities, or any sort of so-called chemical imbalance is at the root of ADD. It's safe to say that ADD is caused by a confluence of natural predisposition and environmental factors.

What should a parent look for as warning signs of ADD? In a child of seven or eight years old, the persistence of:

- The inability to pay or sustain attention
- Chronic disorganization (e.g., in the child's room, homework, activities, and studies in a school setting)
- The inability to listen (which may appear to be disobedience, but isn't)

- The inability to sustain or follow through on tasks requiring prolonged mental effort
- Distractibility
- Always losing things
- Constant fidgeting, running, climbing, and not being able to stay in one place too long (often evident as early as age one)
- Talking too much
- The inability to engage in quiet leisurely activities
- Blurting out answers, not waiting his/her turn, interrupting

WHAT TO DO

1. Consult a child psychiatrist for diagnosis. If you see several of the above symptoms before the age of seven, especially if the symptoms are present in more than one setting—school, home, friends' houses, clubs, athletics—it's possible that your child may suffer from ADD, but it's not definite. A child may have other problems the symptoms of which resemble those of ADD; for example, children who have a behavior disorder, are overly anxious, have been abused, or (in rare cases) suffer from a more serious pervasive developmental disorder, all can manifest symptoms that may look like ADD. The rare manic child is also confused with the child with attention deficit disorder. In most cases, however, a child with ADD usually has enough of the warning signs that the diagnosis isn't too difficult to make. Remember that these children are often of normal intelligence and are not "bad kids." They suffer from a bona fide disorder over which they have little or no control. Rejection and

misunderstanding simply compound problems caused by ADD, which is another reason why early diagnosis and compassionate treatment are so essential. Intelligence and achievement tests will also be important to rule out learning disorders.

2. Once the diagnosis has been confirmed, there are many treatment options available that can ameliorate the child's suffering and improve the whole family situation. Once again, early treatment of this disorder can prevent many far more severe ramifications in adolescence and adulthood. Treatment includes:

- Parent education (this is the most important component)

- The use of stimulant medication, including Ritalin and other drugs. These drugs are extremely useful but should never be used in the absence of other interventions. Sometimes there are mild side effects, but these are far outweighed by the potential for benefit.

- Family therapy

- Cognitive/behavioral therapy

- Special remediation

- Skills training

SEE ALSO

BEHAVIOR DISORDERS   ALL TYPES OF THERAPY
LEARNING DISABILITIES   CHILD PHYSICAL ABUSE
ANXIETY   SEXUAL ABUSE
DEPRESSION AND MANIA   DOES MY CHILD
PSYCHOTROPIC MEDICATION   NEED TESTING?
   AND CHILDREN

LEARNING AND SCHOOL

CHAPTER TWENTY-THREE

Learning Disorders

"Kate does so well in certain aptitude tests, but she fails so miserably in her classwork. I've tried to get her to buckle down and work harder, but she's still getting C's and D's on her report card. I know she's not stupid. Is she just lazy?"

Learning disorders are far more common than had once been thought. While their frequency and variety is understandably distressing, the good news is that the more we know about them, the more we are learning how to treat them, and the less we blame children unfairly for deficiencies that in many cases they can't control. Children who were once labeled stupid or lazy because they couldn't read, write, do mathematics, or process information according to some assumed normal standard now more often are seen to be struggling with specific learning challenges that can benefit from a variety of treatments.

Learning depends upon the mastery of three different processes: input, integration, and output. Input has to do with the child's ability to take in information—for example, to understand words written on the blackboard or absorb the teacher's instructions about how to multiply and divide. The inability to understand words or numbers or instructions may stem from a problem in the central nervous system (such as dyslexia) that impedes the child's visual and cognitive perceptions. Integration involves the ability to call up relevant information or sequential processes the child has already learned. A child with a learning disorder that affects integration may not be able to remember that you add a column of three-digit numbers from the right, not the left. Output involves the expression of language or appropriate use of the body to convey what the child knows; a child with a learning disability that affects output may have difficulty writing legibly.

These information-processing problems (arguably a more accurate term than *learning disabilities*) result in the most common general roadblocks children face in school: reading, writing, and mathematics disorders. Motor skill disorders (fine or gross motor dysfunction, such as awkwardness in the limbs or clumsy manipulation of the fingers) and social emotional disorder (where the child may be unable to empathize with or understand the feelings of other children) may emanate from a deficiency in one or more of these crucial learning processes as well. Learning disorders are also often associated with other syndromes that have a neurological underpinning, such as Tourette's syndrome, seizures, and language disorders.

Delays or difficulties in the development of motor skills, problems with speaking, and/or impairment in cognitive abilities in even very young children may be important omens of learning disabilities. Such indications should not be ignored, for the more quickly the child is diagnosed with a learning disorder, the sooner the child can receive appropriate treatment and preparation for school—which should ward off a good deal of future misery.

This misery commonly stems not only from the learning-disordered child's incapacity to register and process information in the classroom, but also from the emotional and social problems the disorder usually creates for the child secondarily. These children frequently feel and are labeled abnormal, stupid, incompetent, and socially backward—problems that typically intensify the longer the disorder remains undiagnosed. Interestingly, the great majority of children who suffer from learning disorders have at least average intelligence and may in fact (like Kate in the quote that begins this chapter) achieve above-average scores on aptitude tests that focus on areas not affected by the child's particular disorder. However, to compensate emotionally for areas of deficiency, the child may feel compelled to be the class clown, act out defiantly, or disrupt or distract the teacher or other classmates in order to interfere with schoolwork that the child knows he or she cannot easily do. This is especially common with children with attention deficit disorder (some studies indicate that an astonishing 75 percent of all such children may suffer from learning disorders). Hyperactive and impulsive to begin with, children with ADD may employ their natural surfeit of energy to disrupt the class and draw attention to themselves that they feel they can't get in any more acceptable way. Family distress and disapproval of the misbehaving or academically backward son or daughter also commonly intensify emotional problems for the learning-disabled child. Anxiety, depression, low self-esteem, and isolation are the sad lot of many of these children.

Because early diagnosis is so important, it's essential that parents be sensitive to the warning signs of learning disorders. The major symptom consists of a discrepancy between the child's achievement and his or her intelligence (witness Kate). It's not that all such discrepancies are the result of learning disorders—more purely social, emotional, or family issues may be at fault—but they are at least an indication that the child should be tested for learning disabilities. Children also have different styles of learning and greater and lesser aptitudes for certain kinds of learning, none of which necessarily indicates a diagnosable disorder. However, again, testing for these information-processing problems is now sophisticated and thorough enough to indicate what the source of a learning problem more than likely is. Whether to diagnose a learning disability or to rule it out, testing should be done whenever a child demonstrates a discrepancy between aptitude and achievement.

As much as we have discovered about learning disorders, particularly with regard to treating them, their definitive cause continues to elude us. We do know that to some degree they run in families, which suggests that they may be inherited. There are some indications that "wiring" in the brain is slightly different in the learning-disordered child, but because brain chemistry is so complicated and incompletely understood, again nothing definitive can be said. Some risk factors have been suggested but not proven in certain cases of learning-disordered children, such as the mother's use of drugs or alcohol during pregnancy, a difficult delivery, or a low birth weight. However, as mysterious as the causes of learning disabilities may be, great strides have been made in their treatment. That is where the parents of the learning-disabled child are best advised to place their focus and energy.

WHAT TO DO

1. If you notice any of the signs listed above—motor skill difficulty, developmental delays, difficulty speaking— even in very young children, have them tested as soon as possible by a professional certified in learning disabilities.

2. Look for any discrepancies in your children between intelligence and achievement. This means that the most important tests you can have administered to your child should assess intelligence and achievement.

3. If there have been continuous complaints from your child's teacher about school difficulties, consider that the problem may be a learning disability and not simply a problem with the child's discipline or willpower. Do not automatically punish a child for doing poorly in school. Compassion and patience are the watchwords.

4. Remember that learning disabilities are lifelong and treatment will probably be necessary throughout the child's entire schooling—high school and college as well as the earlier grades.

5. If a learning disability is diagnosed, you should work closely with your school system to make sure that your child is in the correct class or receiving adequate and appropriate attention. A special education class may be necessary. A parent's participation is essential, however, because there are often many exercises the learning-disabled child must follow at home, not only in the classroom. This means that the parent has to be as aware as possible of what the child needs so appropriate help can be offered.

SEE ALSO

ATTENTION DEFICIT DISORDER   DEPRESSION AND MANIA
SHOULD MY CHILD BE TESTED?   TICS (INCLUDING TOURETTE'S
ALL TYPES OF THERAPY   SYNDROME)
ANXIETY   INTELLIGENCE

CHAPTER TWENTY-FOUR

Intelligence

"No one in either my family or my wife's family has ever scored this low on an IQ test, Doctor—we're beside ourselves! Is Brad mentally deficient? Did we do something wrong? My wife smoked a bit when she was pregnant—did that wreak havoc on Brad's chromosomes or something? Is there any remedial help we can give him?"

Brad's father is hardly the first parent to call me because of panic at a lower-than-hoped-for score on a child's IQ test. But I did wonder at his urgency: Had his son scored somewhere far below the normal range? In that case, his concern might be legitimate. Then he told me what the score was: 128—a good number of notches *above* average. Evidently Brad's dad thought anything less than 140 signaled intellectual disaster. An Ivy League grad and college professor himself, this gentleman believed that testable intelligence was perhaps the most important marker of status and predictor of future success one could have—as it seems to be for so many parents who call me with similar desperation about what they perceive to be their underperforming kids.

Testable intelligence tells only part of the story, however. In fact, *intelligence* is a broad term under whose umbrella are many skills and aptitudes and capacities, not all of them detectable by standardized tests, but all of which tend to grow in children at fairly predictable rates and developmental stages. These include the use of memory, the ability to differentiate and perceive things in the environment, the ability to see patterns and to register and respond appropriately to stimuli, and finally the capacity for abstract thinking—to sort out, deduce, and generalize about things.

Huge strides in intelligence are made in the first year of life as children bond with their caretakers and perform various experiments to see the differing effects their actions have on objects and people in their environment. The ability to communicate expands explosively in the first year, from inchoate crying to the miracle of the baby's first words. By somewhere in the second year, symbolic thinking has developed in children and, with this, the ability to solve various problems and involve oneself in imaginative play. Language development proceeds at a swift pace toward full comprehension and expression—certainly by the time school begins. Indeed, language development correlates reliably with the overall development of intelligence. All aspects of intelligence continue to expand as a child goes through the preschool and school years; in language and patterns of knowledge, simplicity yields to complexity. There may be nothing more thrilling to us as parents than to see all these aspects of intelligence interact to produce a child who's able to function in the outside world with the wide spectrum of curiosity, understanding, and knowledge of the normal child.

The origins of intelligence are hotly debated. How much is genetic and how much is the product of environment may never be entirely known. However, since we can't (yet) do much about a child's genes, we tend to concentrate on the controllable component of the equation, the environment, and indeed it is clear that environmental influences have a profound effect on improving or impeding a child's overall intelligence. However, assessing improvement or impediment is (as Brad's father needs to be reminded) a very difficult task, because no one test—or possibly no combination of tests—can tell us anything definitive. The intellectual quotient or IQ test is most often used to measure a child's intelligence, and there are also more specific tests that focus on particular years of life, starting in the first year, to measure developmentally appropriate intelligence. While performance on these standardized tests does seem somewhat to predict how a child will do in school, we also know that IQ tests do not reflect a number of other crucial components. Creativity, certain kinds of intuitive ingenuity, artistic ability, and emotional sensitivity to other people also are part of the mix of intelligence, and yet often these do not register significantly (or at all) on standardized aptitude tests, which tend to favor the cognitive over the intuitive. (A playwright, artist, musician, or philosopher we may rightly label a genius may not have done all that well on an IQ test or an SAT exam.) In addition, standardized tests do not take into account the physical, emotional, and mental states of the child at the time of testing, or the ability to function in a test-taking situation. However, because tests offer up seemingly unquestionable numerical results, they often appear to be definitive, and in our competitive society we rely on them in lieu of having anything more concrete with which to make an assessment.

Fortunately, the great majority of children fall completely in the normal range of intelligence. There are, however, children who fall significantly below it, and once again, this seems to be a product both of genetic and environmental influences. Children whose intelligence is abnormally low also tend to have emotional difficulties—trouble adapting in school, the family, and other social venues. They may suffer from neglect or abuse, or medical, congenital, or genetic reasons and problems may be implicated. The word *retarded* is too often applied indiscriminately to children. Indeed, what we call retardation ranges from borderline to profound, with dramatically different implications for the child's future capacities (a borderline retarded child may well grow up to have a normal, satisfying life; the profoundly retarded child will probably always need intensive care). Other people are regarded as subnormally intelligent because of emotional problems—depression, anger, and passive-aggressiveness may interfere with the child's ability to learn, take tests, and interact socially in the ways schools require of them. Learning disabilities, which are far more common than once had been thought, will also interfere with an assessment of intelligence, once again often leading to misguidedly pessimistic notions of a child's real capacities. Receptive and/or expressive language difficulty as well as attention deficit disorder all will interfere with the child's ability to take standardized examinations. Thus there should be great wariness in both parents and educators about coming to any firm conclusions based on the outcome of an IQ test.

WHAT TO DO

1. Remember that the overwhelming odds are that your child has normal intelligence. There is little special you have to do to encourage the development of your child's intelligence other than provide a nurturing, physically healthy, and socially interactive environment. It is known that the more you interact and create appropriate social bonding opportunities for your child, beginning in infancy, the more fully developed his or her intelligence will be.

2. Always focus on your child's unique strengths and try not to compare your child's intelligence to that of siblings or other parents' children. Such comparisons not only whittle away at self-esteem, but they increase anxiety—which decreases the development of curiosity and intelligence. In the realm of intelligence, comparisons truly are odious.

3. Stimulate your child's curiosity. Curiosity remains one of the best indicators of a child's intellectual and emotional development. Stimulate language and reading skills as much as possible by talking with your

child from early on, listening and responding to your child, and reading to your child. Show by example that you regard reading and other intellectual pursuits as a pleasure—an even greater pleasure than television. Doing this in addition to limiting your child's television time will make reading and learning seem less of a punishment and more of an opportunity to attend to even more interesting pursuits.

4. Make sure your child is socially involved, because healthy interaction with other people has a direct impact on intelligence. Social groups, sports, and school activities all help to expand your child's intellectual as well as social capacities.

5. Remember that in the absence of other signs and symptoms of developmental delay related to such milestones as walking, talking, toilet training, and the like, it is highly unlikely that your child is mentally retarded.

6. Recognize the limits of IQ and other tests, and focus on the unique confluence of talents and abilities that your child brings to the world. That is what will help your child flourish in life.

7. If your child exhibits signs of developmental milestone delay in such areas as crawling, smiling, talking, walking, toilet training, and separation ability, professional consultation and possibly developmental testing should be pursued.

SEE ALSO

LEARNING DISORDERS   DOES MY CHILD NEED TESTING?
THE UNDERACHIEVER   DEPRESSION AND MANIA
ATTENTION DEFICIT DISORDER ANGER
LANGUAGE DISORDERS

Chapter Twenty-five
School Phobia

"I don't care what you do to me! I'm not going! You can't make me!"

Fear of school afflicts many children at different times. Usually it's relatively fleeting—a feared test, teacher, bully, or class assignment can be enough to halt a child in his or her tracks. Few of us don't have memories of praying for snow days or to get sick so we wouldn't have to go to school on this or that particular day. Some of us even managed to hoodwink our parents into thinking we were sick. But most children grit their teeth and go through with it, even if they hate it.

Other children are far more intransigent. School phobia should not be confused with truancy, which generally means that the child lets his/her parents think he or she is going to school and then takes the day off. Truancy is a behavioral problem, not a phobia. School phobia proceeds from an obvious and entrenched fear, and children with this problem generally won't get out of bed or leave the house no matter what punishment is in store. For them, staying home and near their parents is the only way they can imagine to decrease anxiety. It's not that they won't go to school; they feel as if they can't.

School phobia can appear at any age, but it tends to increase in frequency as adolescence approaches. Although school phobia appears to happen abruptly (the child may well have been able to go to school all year with no problem, and then suddenly be unable to go), in fact there appear to be pre-phobic signs that indicate its imminence. Stressful times in the home, at school, or in the child's play group can be the forerunner of full-blown school phobia, as can moving to a new neighborhood, switching into a new school, having an illness, or even having a learning disorder. Anything that prevents a child from going to school (such as a long-term physical illness or disability) can precipitate school phobia in children prone to it.

The fear of going to school varies from mild and vague—as with children who drag their feet in the morning and almost miss the bus, or who make general statements about not liking a particular teacher or classmate or class—to angry and overt refusals accompanied by all-out rage, hostility, panic, and threats of (sometimes even attempts at) suicide. Sometimes children will run away if forced to go to school. These resistances tend to be worse on Mondays and early in the day, when apprehensiveness is highest. After a while, the school-phobic child experiences tremendous shame and humiliation about not being like everybody else, and tries to stay away from children who they sense are already aware of their "problem." Thus they end up as social isolates, staying home all day, usually developing a secondary social withdrawal syndrome. School-phobic children not only are typically anxious, but frequently become depressed as well. Some experts say that school phobia is actually one minor symptom in a child who is suffering from anxiety and depression in general. Generally, children who are school-phobic have always tended to be more dependent on their parents and families, and indeed become overly dependent when the school phobia takes over their lives.

WHAT TO DO

1. The most important fact for a parent to know about school phobia is that the earlier the child can be induced to go back to school, the better it will be for

him or her. Unfortunately, knowing this does not make the parent's task easier. Children who are school-phobic aren't simply frightened. They often suffer from panic and are full of irrational fears of school that generally won't go away even with the most patient and rational argument. Second, it is common for parents of school-phobic children to back off because of their fear of their angry and resistant kids; they don't want to upset the child more, possibly because they themselves have unresolved phobic issues. They may sometimes join the child in blaming the school, teachers, and/or other classmates for what is really an internal anxiety in the child.

2. To get the child back to school, we often have to help the child to feel s/he has some sense of control. For example, let the child determine what day s/he is going to try to go back to class, and/or how many hours s/he will try to stay in school, and/or the means of transport s/he will use to get to school in the morning. Giving a sense of partnership to the child in this process is crucial.

3. Discussion of the advantages of attending school, being with friends, and being involved in school activities helps.

4. Sometimes both parents remaining home in the morning to encourage the child will help the child to feel more secure, as may giving the child a picture to take to school of parents, the home, a brother or sister, and/or a loved pet.

5. It is crucial that the child perceives that parents are in fact in favor of the child returning to school. This factor can be the determining one in helping the child make the decision to go back; feeling that the parents strongly believe in attending school often eventually bolsters the child's own determination to

please his or her parents. The parents' determination can work on the child's unconscious mind and do more to change the child's outlook than many parents might think.

6. For some particularly resistant children, therapy with a mental health-care professional—individual and family, combined with parental counseling—is called for and can be helpful. Often behavior modification techniques are used.

7. Sometimes a change of school to a special education center that is specifically for school-phobic children may be necessary.

8. Medication, such as antidepressants or mild tranquilizers, may sometimes be helpful. If all of these measures do not work, removal of the child to a day hospital, overnight at a psychiatric hospital, and even boarding school may be necessary to provide the kind of intensive treatment a very small minority of school-phobic children may need.

SEE ALSO

DEPRESSION   PSYCHOTROPIC MEDICATION
ANXIETY   AND CHILDREN
FEARS AND PHOBIAS   ALL TYPES OF THERAPY
SEPARATION ANXIETY   THE UNDERACHIEVER
BEHAVIOR DISORDER

Chapter Twenty-six

The Underachiever

"But I'm an English teacher. My husband's a newspaper editor. All our other children were reading by age five. Why is Johnny so backward?"

The second most common reason parents consult me is underachievement. (The first is children who misbehave.) A child who performs below par in the classroom is such a major source of worry to parents because so many see school performance as the clearest yardstick of their child's development and future prospects. It's often also a matter of status. Many parents react to their children's report cards as if they were as much an assessment of the parents' own ability, intelligence, and family standing as they are of their kids' skills at spelling or arithmetic. This anxious, vicarious participation in the child's life can be extreme—witness the mothers and fathers who worry about their toddlers getting into the "right" Harvard-track nursery school.

Nervous questions abound, fueled by dire-sounding conditions we hear about in the media: "Does my child have attention deficit disorder?" "Is he mentally retarded?" "Is she not doing well because we got divorced?" "Is there something wrong with his hearing?" "Am I not pushing Jackie enough?" "Am I requiring too much of Mary?" "Is Ronnie dyslexic?" In fact, underachievement in school can have many causes. It's a huge and complicated subject, and the first advice I offer any worried parent is simply not to jump to conclusions about what the problem may be. Buzzword disabilities—for example, attention deficit disorder—are often prematurely blamed. There are many kinds of learning disorders with varying degrees of severity, and many options for their treatment. There may be physical problems with sight or hearing that impede the child's ability to learn. Emotional problems, behavioral disorders, family difficulties, and sexual or physical abuse may also be at the root of a child's diminished or limited capacity to take in and process information. Sometimes a child may do well in certain areas and not in others simply because s/he has greater talent in one subject than s/he has in another. Once again, parental pressure and expectations—"Your daddy always got A's in math! Why are you having such a problem with it?"—may lead to false assumptions about a child's "disability." It may take some time before children with a true difficulty can be diagnosed and treated; even the experts can't always pinpoint the problem right off.

This section offers a general overview of the common causes of underachievement. Consult the chapters that deal separately with each of these diagnoses and conditions as you deem appropriate. But most of all, be patient. Discovering what may be impeding your child's ability to read or write or calculate will probably take some careful investigation. Underachievement is what is called "a common final pathway" for many different problems that may not be readily apparent.

Adequate diagnosis of learning disorders involves special testing done by psychological experts certified in this particular field. Certainly the child who is hyperactive, inattentive, and impulsive—and consequently not doing well in school—may have attention deficit disorder and require a multifaceted treatment, including use of a stimulant medication, social skills therapy, and special remediation. Children may suffer from different learning disabilities that interfere with their capacity specifically to write and read, or do mathematics. Other children do poorly in the classroom because they suffer from behavior disorders, which, while not specifically learning disabilities, are disruptive conditions that certainly interfere with the child's willingness to learn, act appropriately, or follow a teacher's directions. Children with these behavior disorders commonly need much more intensive psychological treatment and monitoring (sometimes involving family therapy, special schools, and/or residential placement) than those who suffer only from learning disabilities, which can often be dealt with by purely educational techniques. Tourette's syndrome, because of its disruptiveness and the social alienation it causes, also interferes with learning and performance. Rarer psychological conditions such as pervasive developmental disorder, for which poor performance in school is often the first symptom, may also be a cause, as may mental retardation (the diagnosis of which depends on a complete physical examination, family history, and psychological testing) and borderline intellectual functioning (indicated by an IQ between 70 and 85). Children with a developmental delay—who usually have difficulty in one area but not in others—are sometimes misdiagnosed as retarded when in fact they often will catch up in the deficient area; it just takes them longer to do so.

Emotional problems may also be at the root of poor performance. Not surprisingly, children who perform poorly in class and can't keep up with their peers often suffer from low self-esteem and depression and may become school-phobic. However, it's important to consider that the phobia may stem from an undiagnosed physical condition or learning disability, not (as parents may think) because of laziness, disobedience, or willfulness. The child may blame the school, other classmates, or the teacher as the reason s/he hates going when the real problem may be very different. It is essential to get the school-phobic child back into school as quickly as possible, but accomplishing this may depend upon making sure that the child be tested first for learning disabilities. Similarly, depression may be the cause or a symptom of learning difficulties and must be looked at carefully. Differentiating between the learning-disabled child who has become depressed and the depressed child who has difficulty learning depends on looking for other symptoms of depression besides poor school performance (e.g., a persistently sad mood, irritability, loss of pleasure in social activities, isolation). If the child functions well in other spheres, the likelihood is that his or her poor performance is due to a learning disability and that the depression is symptomatic. Other emotional problems associated with learning difficulties may stem from chaos and disorganization in the child's home life, or chronic fighting between parents or siblings. Children from single-parent and stepparent families seem to do less well in school, although the exact reason is not known. While divorce per se does not seem to be the cause of underachievement, the conflict and insecurity surrounding divorce—and the family's reactions to it—may have a negative impact on the child's academic performance.

Physical disability and poor health also commonly have a profound impact on the child's ability to learn. Hearing and sight should be checked regularly. The child may suffer from mild seizures that go unnoticed or are misperceived as momentary inattention or fatigue; these are petit mal or psychomotor seizures rather than the more dramatic grand mal seizures that most people more typically associate with epilepsy. Children in poor health may not feel the motivation or have the stamina to sustain attention in school. Asthma, diabetes, and migraine headaches commonly have a negative impact on a child's learning capacity, and problems can also result from the medications the child may be taking for these conditions, such as a common one for asthma, which in some children causes hyperactive symptoms that mimic ADD and in others causes grogginess. Rarer neurological conditions such as narcolepsy (a seizure that causes the child suddenly to fall asleep) may also be at fault.

A mismatch between the child and school may also be at fault. Some teachers aren't trained to recognize and deal with special children, gifted children, children from unfamiliar cultures, or children with different learning styles. Gifted children sometimes don't achieve well for an additional reason: The parental pressure put upon them to achieve, to live up to their potential, may be stifling. They may feel they are always falling short and thus may simply give up. They may also not want to appear different from their peers, so they strive to seem less intelligent, talented, or competent than they are.

WHAT TO DO

1. Make sure your child is in good physical health and receives a regular complete medical checkup, including thorough examinations of sight and hearing.

2. Parents should discuss underachievement issues with school personnel to make sure that they understand the problem as the school perceives it.

3. Investigate and make sure that your child is tested by appropriate experts (in learning disabilities, intelligence, education, etc.) in school performance.

4. If your child appears depressed or anxious, consult a mental health professional.

5. Like any other symptom of a child's distress, underachievement should be treated with compassion and respect and without harsh criticism. Remember that many underlying causes may be at the root of the problem and that the child is more than likely suffering from secondary emotional and social problems. Also be reassured that many effective options for treatment are available to you and your child.

SEE ALSO

BEHAVIOR DISORDERS

ATTENTION DEFICIT DISORDER

LEARNING DISORDERS

OBSESSIVE-COMPULSIVE
   DISORDER

ANXIETY

DEPRESSION AND MANIA

PERVASIVE DEVELOPMENTAL
   DISORDER (AUTISM)

PSYCHOTROPIC MEDICATION
   AND CHILDREN

SLEEP DISORDERS

INTELLIGENCE

SCHOOL PHOBIA

DOES MY CHILD NEED
   TESTING?

THE PHYSICALLY ILL CHILD

TICS (INCLUDING TOURETTE'S
   SYNDROME)

CHILD PHYSICAL ABUSE

SEXUAL ABUSE

THE BODY

Chapter Twenty-seven
Stuttering

"I sit there in agony listening to Bill try to talk. I just don't know what to do."

Learning to talk is a bit like learning to walk. Children accomplish both at their own pace, encountering different triumphs and setbacks along the way. Some march sturdily across the living room floor into Mommy's or Daddy's arms with barely a hitch; others collapse crying into a heap at the third wobbly step. Similarly, some children take to speech with greater ease and speed than others, who struggle more to sort out and articulate these strange new sounds called words. Stuttering—an impairment in fluency characterized by many repetitions of consonants and vowel sounds and/or prolongations of syllables—is a common form of this struggle.

Sometimes the stutterer's speech is completely blocked; at other times there is mild or moderate hesitation. Most stuttering begins in early childhood and peaks somewhere between the ages of three and four and a half. Boys stutter three times more frequently than girls. The good news is that more than 99 percent of children don't stutter by the time they are teenagers. For that unfortunate small percentage destined to be chronic stutterers, the speech impairment generally is clearly evident by the elementary school years and often does not improve appreciably over time—although even for chronic stutterers fluency may wane and wax at periods of greater and lesser anxiety. It's not surprising that most stutterers become very tense, often choosing their words carefully to avoid difficult sounds, and sometimes refusing to speak altogether.

There are many theories about what causes stuttering. Some consider it a neurotic disorder; others see it as emanating from family conflicts. Recent studies seem to indicate that the root cause may be biological. The neck muscles and laryngeal muscles in many stutterers appear to be different from those in nonstutterers. Stutterers usually have relatives who also stutter—another indication that the physical susceptibility may be genetically inherited. Although anxiety clearly makes stuttering worse, it does not appear to be its root cause.

However, inherited or not, stuttering nearly always causes secondary emotional problems. Little is more excruciating for a child than to stand up in front of a snickering class to give a book report and not be able to get a word out. Other children frequently shun, mimic, or otherwise make merciless fun of the stutterer. Because the child cannot easily engage with other children verbally, social development is often impaired. The stutterer's anxiety, shame, and humiliation not only eat away at any positive sense of self, sometimes leading to depression, but also exacerbate the stuttering. Family anxiety, criticism, and pressure can intensify the problem as well. Most parents want their children to be normal in every way, but particularly in language expression. The child may think stuttering is his or her fault, or may feel stupid or weak or incompetent at having no control over his or her speech— all of which just makes the stuttering worse than before.

WHAT TO DO

1. If your child shows signs of stuttering, as many children will when they first learn to speak, don't leap to correct the child or in any other way react with tension or disapproval. Just ignore the problem. Let the child work the word or sound out him- or herself. Remember that 99 percent of children will not stut-

ter by the time they get through childhood. Stuttering is almost always destined to be temporary.

2. For the same reason, don't supply the word to the stuttering child, as tempting as this may be.

3. Requiring the child to speak fluently never works. Attempting to discipline the child out of a stuttering block does nothing but worsen the stuttering.

4. If your child's stuttering persists or intensifies over time, it is certainly advisable to consult a speech therapist who will test your child for any possible contributing learning or physical difficulties and, if indicated, provide therapy that is usually very helpful in assisting the child to navigate blocks to speech.

5. If your child suffers particularly acutely from emotional problems caused by stuttering, it may be wise to consult a mental health-care professional—and possibly investigate family therapy as well—to ease the child's anxiety and bolster feelings of self-worth.

6. Tell your child about Winston Churchill, whose lifelong struggle with stuttering didn't prevent him from becoming one of the greatest orators of all time.

SEE ALSO

ANXIETY

DEPRESSION AND MANIA

LANGUAGE DISORDERS

DOES MY CHILD
NEED TESTING?

ALL TYPES OF THERAPY

CHAPTER TWENTY-EIGHT
Children Who
Don't Speak

"Come on, Janey, we've had enough of this nonsense. The nice doctor is just asking you how old you are. Janey? Janey! What's wrong with you? Answer him this minute!"

The frustrated nudge from Janey's mother is one she finds herself repeating with her daughter every time they go out of the house and Janey is expected to speak. Nine-year-old Janey has no problem talking with her parents and brother and sister at home. But when she walks out the door, she shuts down—and shuts up.

Sharon, a six-year-old girl who came to see me a while back, sat in the waiting room with her mother and little brother and talked so loudly I could hear her through my office door. But when I invited her into my office, she became silent—and remained that way throughout our session, even though she looked alert, bright, and even interested in my many questions.

What Sharon and Janey exhibit is called selective mutism. Such children may not speak to anyone outside the home or at school, or just won't talk to adults other than at least one of her/his parents. When they do speak at home, in the majority of cases their language and speech are perfectly normal. For a variety of reasons, they carefully select those with whom they will interact verbally, and they cannot be made to talk to anyone else.

Close observation of selectively mute children and detailed histories acquired from their parents usually reveal that they have always been timid, shy, and withdrawn and that they tend to isolate themselves from any social interaction. Some cling to their mothers. Others have irrational fears (phobias) of everyday situations. Some also exhibit repetitive compulsive habits. On the whole, children with selective mutism have always appeared a bit socially backward or immature compared to their peers. Many have wetting and soiling problems as well.

While these children have generally always been quiet, their mutism usually starts out slowly and then insidiously enlarges. Only in rare cases does the mutism start out dramatically, and when it does, there is usually a clear cause: a sudden stressful situation such as sexual or physical abuse, the death of a close friend or family member, or other forced separation from loved ones. Many children who live in foster care exhibit selective mutism because of neglect and/or abuse as well as the trauma of dislocating from their original families and homes.

As inexplicable as selective mutism may at first appear, my experience treating such children is that, by spending enough time with the child and sensitively interviewing his/her family and/or caretakers, the underpinnings of the condition almost always become readily apparent. It may take patience to get at these root causes, but typically they involve family dysfunction, such as having a parent who is depressed or otherwise unable to supply the child with normal nurturing and emotional sustenance, or one of the traumas already mentioned.

WHAT TO DO

The most important—and possibly the most difficult—task for the parent of a child who becomes mute outside the house is to keep from looking outside the home for the cause or the solution. Almost always the cause is rooted in the home, not outside of it. This dramatic symptom should serve as a sign that you need to explore the inner workings of your own family, with special attention given to the child's relations with each family member. Ask the following questions:

1. Has the child reacted traumatically to an event that you considered unimportant (e.g., a best friend moving away, or the death of a pet)?

2. Are there any indications that the child has been abused?

3. Is the family atmosphere particularly tense or difficult? Has there been unemployment, drinking, mourning, or excessive anger?

4. Does the child appear to feel guilty about something?

5. Are Mom and Dad arguing so violently that the child feels they might separate?

Such questions aren't always easy or pleasant to consider, but they often hold the key to unexplored areas of your child's experience and distress. Dealing directly and reassuringly with the child about the problem is the surest way to the symptom's remission.

Whatever its cause, most children with selective mutism get better by the age of ten. If it lasts much longer than this, the prognosis becomes much more serious. Certainly if selective mutism lasts longer than several months and you have tried repeatedly to observe and question your child and discuss with him or her all issues that may be affecting him or her, but you have had no success, then a consultation with a trained mental health-care provider is in order. There is a high rate of success with one or more of the following treatments:

• Individual psychotherapy
• Family psychotherapy

- Speech therapy for some children who also have speech problems
- Antidepressant medications

It is also important for a professional to rule out other possible diagnoses that could present as a child not speaking or doing so with great difficulty, such as mental retardation, deafness, pervasive developmental disorder, or a language disorder.

SEE ALSO

ANXIETY

FEARS AND PHOBIAS

ENURESIS (WETTING)

ENCOPRESIS (SOILING)

LANGUAGE DISORDERS

ARTICULATION DISORDER

CHILD PHYSICAL ABUSE

SEXUAL ABUSE

INTELLIGENCE

ALL TYPES OF THERAPY

OBSESSIVE-COMPULSIVE
    DISORDER

SHYNESS

CHILDREN OF DEPRESSED
    PARENTS

PSYCHOTROPIC MEDICATION
    AND CHILDREN

PERVASIVE DEVELOPMENTAL
    DISORDER (AUTISM)

CHAPTER TWENTY-NINE

Language Disorders

"Bobby's two? But he's so quiet! When my little Susie was that age, she was talking a blue streak!"

There are few moments more joyful for parents than hearing their child say his or her first word. Language obviously unites parent and child in new, exhilarating ways; it's almost as if children become "real people" when they start to speak. It's common—and can be a lot of fun—to keep a diary or record book of when Susie or Bobby first says "Mama" or "Dada," or of what words they know by the time they're twelve months old. Indeed, language skills—when they first appear and as they evolve—are also important hallmarks of a child's social, emotional, and cognitive development.

However, because of many parents' perceived notions of what is supposed to happen when, it's common for them to worry when their little one doesn't appear to be on the "right" (i.e., someone else's) verbal schedule. As a result, what may start out as a joyous celebratory record of Susie or Bobby's first words sometimes evolves into a worrisome report card full of Mom and Dad's anxieties about why one child hasn't started talking or doesn't know as many words at as early an age as another.

The welcome news is that such anxieties are almost always unwarranted. While the development of language (like that of any fundamental skill) has certain characteristics common to all children at roughly similar ages and intervals, it is also a unique process that varies with each individual. Children navigate their ways into language at different rates, exhibiting various traits and characteristics peculiar to each little girl and boy. The reasons for these variations range from inborn biological causes to any number of outside environmental influences. But the basic reassuring fact is that over 95 percent of all children use language effectively and satisfactorily by the age of five—even though few experience no bumps along the road.

The important point is that what's normal for one child isn't necessarily normal for another. Observe your child's rates of development to see what's normal for him or her. From very early on, you saw how s/he first used words, how s/he gestured to make his or her language clear, how s/he responded to the words and ideas of others. Your judgments are the ones that count, and in the rare instances where a child may have a language skill problem requiring professional treatment, the insights and observations you provide will offer invaluable information in determining that treatment.

We don't know all the variables that account for individual differences in language development, but we do know that early verbal and nonverbal environments play important roles. As you might expect, children who are spoken to a lot and who enjoy physically and emotionally healthy environments tend to develop at optimal rates verbally. Speak more to a child, keep tension down and anxiety at bay in the home, and s/he will probably flourish, speaking earlier and with more fluency than s/he otherwise would. Good language skills signal more than verbal aptitude or ability—they're the sign of a healthy home environment.

Having said there is no one "normal" timetable of development for everybody, I will nonetheless offer some very general guidelines that give you at least a ballpark idea of what to expect when. Remember that most glitches or delays in this schedule generally take care of themselves.

- Most children smile by two to three months, coo by three and a half months, respond to voices by five months, and babble by six months.

- By ten to twelve months, children may know a few (two or three) words, and by three and a half to five years, thousands.

- By two years, most children can string together a two-word sentence; by three, a three-word sentence.

- By four years old, children can use a variety of simple sentence forms.

- By five, 95 percent of children experience few or no problems with language expression and understanding.

How to Tell If There's a Problem

What about the 5 percent who do experience impairments in language development? We'll go over various possible causes for such difficulties in a moment, but first there is a general list of warning signs to look out for:

- The child can speak only very few words by eighteen or nineteen months.

- The child apparently has no understanding of the language by eighteen months.

- The child has odd or unusual language problems (e.g., chronically peculiar syntax or pronoun use, consistently leaving out certain words or using the wrong ones) that persist after eighteen months.

- The child can't point to body parts by twenty months.

- The child cannot put together any sentences at all by the age of two and a half.

- The child experiences persistent articulation problems (e.g., speaking in a slow or abnormal way) after the age of four and a half.

In response to these signs, a professional will first seek to rule out major—and generally rare—biological causes that can interfere with language development, such as congenital deafness; chronic infections that may cause temporary, partial, or complete deafness; congenital brain abnormalities; and acquired neurological problems. Children with psychiatric problems tend to suffer a higher incidence of language difficulties, although we don't always know which came first and may have caused the other. There seem to be certain negative environmental influences associated with language disorders, such as poverty, poor nutrition, parental neglect or physical abuse, prenatal exposure to alcohol and cocaine, being born late in the family, and being part of a large family. Unfortunately, there are few definitive ways to determine what is the product of external influence and what may be a subtle brain abnormality that we are unable to detect or monitor on X rays or scans.

When the above serious causes for language problems are ruled out—as they usually are—the two remaining diagnostic categories into which children with language difficulties fall are specific expressive language disorder and mixed expressive and receptive disorder. The first has to do with the child's ability to communicate (speaking in a slow or abnormal way, etc.); the second adds to this problem difficulty in understanding others. Each of these disorders is sometimes accompanied by articulation problems or stuttering as well.

WHAT TO DO

1. First of all, parents should understand that language acquisition doesn't occur in isolation from other factors such as healthy physical living conditions and family relations. Children under stress from whatever source are at risk for developmental interference, and some of the first signs of this interference will appear in the realm of language. As suggested, talk to your children warmly and often, and make sure that they

are not the victims of undue stress or chaos in the home. Ask them questions and allow them to express themselves freely. This is the matrix out of which good communication and language skills grow.

2. Professional interventions that are necessary in cases of children who exhibit persistent problems in language acquisition, use, or development:

   • Physical and neurological evaluations (be sure that the mouth, neck muscles, and nerves are examined)

   • Hearing test

   • Psychological tests to rule out commonly occurring learning disabilities as well as to get a measure of intelligence

   • Speech and language tests

   • Psychiatric evaluation by a child psychiatrist

3. Recommended treatments include:

   • Therapy by a certified speech/language professional, either individually or in groups

   • Parent counseling if parenting issues appear to be causative

   • Psychiatric therapy if indicated

   • Learning disability treatment by a remediation specialist if learning disorders have been diagnosed

SEE ALSO

INTELLIGENCE   STUTTERING
CHILDREN WHO DON'T SPEAK   LEARNING DISORDERS
ARTICULATION DISORDER   ATTENTION DEFICIT DISORDER
PERVASIVE DEVELOPMENTAL   DOES MY CHILD NEED TESTING?
   DISORDER (AUTISM)   ALL TYPES OF THERAPY

CHAPTER THIRTY

Articulation Disorder

*"But she hasn't lost her baby teeth yet, so it can't be that—
I'm so embarrassed for her, Mom! You can't understand
what Peggy's saying with that lisp! And she shortens her
words like a baby. Her teacher thinks she just might be slow
to develop, but every other kid at her nursery school speaks
okay. They're starting to make fun of her. I'm sure she'll
grow out of it, but . . ."*

Many of the problems and conditions addressed in this book
are indeed things that children usually grow out of. Children
all have different developmental timetables, and some stum-
ble at various points where others seem to glide through ef-
fortlessly; this is never more true than with speech and
language development. However, Peggy's mother may well
be wrong in this case; if little Peggy's lisp and word shorten-
ings do signify a bona fide articulation or phonological disorder, she needs professional intervention to help her deal
with it.

Articulation disorders are by far the most common cause
of communication trouble that children have. Up to 20 percent of preschoolers experience some trouble in articulation.
The disorder is officially defined as a failure to produce developmentally appropriate (for age and dialect) speech sounds.
Some children with this disorder substitute one sound for
another (for example, pronouncing *f* instead of *th*), while
others drop syllables, leave off the ends of words, or omit
certain other sounds altogether. Like Peggy, some children's
speech is distorted by a lisp that persists despite the presence
or absence of baby teeth. Some children reverse the order of

sounds in a word. On the whole, many children with this disorder appear to be younger or more socially immature than other children their age.

Most children are diagnosed with this disorder by the time they are four years old, because by that time the average child is able to speak relatively fluently. However, the diagnosis can be made earlier if the disorder is particularly acute or severe. Articulation problems almost always occur in concert with other language disorders (discussed in the previous chapter); it is rare when they don't go hand in hand. This is another good reason why Peggy's mother is well advised to seek help: Her daughter's speech difficulties probably signal other problems that need to be addressed as soon as possible. Also, it is often difficult to distinguish between a language disorder and an articulation disorder; it takes an expert in the field to make this diagnosis and suggest appropriate treatment.

WHAT TO DO

1. If you fear that your child has an articulation disorder, make sure your pediatrician examines the child's mouth to see if there are any morphological problems that may be causing the problem.

2. Hearing problems are sometimes associated with an articulation disorder; thus a hearing test is always important.

3. Have your child's entire speech and language development assessed by an expert (to whom your pediatrician will probably be able to refer you) so that the problem can be seen in the largest context and you can receive the best advice about what specifically can be done to help your child.

4. If your child has this disorder, he or she will need remedial help as soon as possible and will probably need

to continue some form of remediation throughout most of the elementary school years.

5. Not surprisingly, some children with this disorder become very shy and reticent and are unwilling to participate fully in social, family, and school situations. Be as supportive and positive as you can be; above all, do not criticize your child for the mispronunciations or speech difficulties this disorder causes. You may well have to seek psychotherapeutic treatment (one-on-one and/or family therapy) to help your child deal with these secondary emotional problems. Be sure to praise your child for any progress s/he makes socially and speechwise.

SEE ALSO

LANGUAGE DISORDERS	SHYNESS
STUTTERING	DOES MY CHILD NEED TESTING?
ANXIETY	ALL TYPES OF THERAPY

CHAPTER THIRTY-ONE

Enuresis (Wetting)

"I don't know how it happened, Mommy—maybe the roof leaked on my bed when I was asleep!"

We all start out giving pretty direct expression to our hungers, urges, and needs. A baby cries to be fed, coos when she's happy, and if she has to relieve herself, she simply does so (and we thank whoever invented Pampers). Then around age two comes one of the rudest awakenings in any child's life: toilet training. Probably no one navigates this period without suffering at least some resistance, anxiety, or anger, but by the age of three most children learn to use the bathroom anyway. Fortunately, over 90 percent of children are able to control urination by the time they're five years old.

However, for varying reasons, some children just aren't able to control the urge to urinate by this age. Whichever of the two categories of enuretics the child may fall into—primary, which describes children who still can't control urination by age five, or secondary, which refers to children who may have learned to stay dry by age three or four but start wetting their beds or their clothes between ages four and eight—s/he usually suffers terrible shame and embarrassment about it. In fact, the emotional problems associated with enuresis are probably more often caused by other people's—especially parents'—reactions to it than by the child's own reactions. I have seen hundreds of enuretics over the years and have never met one child who would admit to the problem when first asked about it.

While we don't know what causes enuresis in all cases, we do know that secondary enuretics often wet their beds or clothes (nocturnal enuresis is far more common than wetting clothes during the day, a problem known as diurnal enuresis) because of stress—sometimes due to such traumas as the birth of a younger sister or brother, sometimes because of sexual abuse, sometimes because of a physical trauma such as head injury. There is persuasive evidence that a predisposition to enuresis may sometimes be inherited. In rare cases the cause is biological—such as a bladder that cannot handle normal urine volumes, mild muscular defects in the bladder walls, and possibly some variation in what is called circadian rhythms (bodily changes at different times of day and night; for example, the child may not experience the decrease in nighttime urine production that most people do). Some constipated children also seem more prone to wetting. In rare cases, especially in children who wet themselves during the day, there may be a urinary infection or abnormalities of the internal urinary organs. Some psychosocial conditions are associated with enuresis, such as poverty, child neglect, broken homes, single-parent families, poor parenting skills, or institutional living. Children who are mentally retarded or suffer developmental lags in other areas (such as speech, language, and motor function) also tend more than other children to be enuretic, as do impulsive children in general. While we don't think that most enuresis is caused by underlying psychiatric disturbances, it does sometimes accompany certain behavior disorders, habit disorders, and aggression. We also see enuresis more commonly in shy and anxious children.

Enuresis in any of its forms is usually upsetting to parents as well as their children. Some parents have angrily announced to me that they're sure their kids "do it on purpose—just to annoy me!" Whatever the cause of enuresis is found to be, parents need to realize that in the vast majority of cases, the child truly cannot control it. While very occasionally a child may wet the bed on purpose as an act of anger or rebellion or to get attention, these children need just as much understanding, compassion, and patience as in the far more

common case of children who physically cannot help themselves. One thing it's safe to assume: The child suffers terribly, whatever the cause of the enuresis. The anxiety, guilt,
and despair—and the ridicule and ostracism they receive
when they stay overnight at a friend's house or go away to
camp and wet the bed—can truly be unbearable. In fact,
enuresis often leads to secondary difficulties such as avoidance and isolation from other people as well as problems
with schoolwork.

WHAT TO DO

If your child is five years old and wets him/herself at least
several times per week—whether it has always been the case
or has just now started—the following measures should be
taken:

1. Become part of a team with your child and give
   him/her the feeling that the whole family is going to
   try to help him or her overcome this problem.
2. Have your child restrict fluid intake after dinner and
   not drink anything at all for at least two hours before
   retiring.
3. Awaken your child at least once during the night to
   urinate.
4. For nocturnal enuretics (the great majority of bed-
   wetters), tell your child to drink more and more water during the day to help him/her train him/herself
   to control urine volume.
5. Supply your child with a waterproof undersheet.
6. Praise your child for dry nights.

If within a three-month period the above measures do not
work, then professional intervention is necessary and should
include the following:

1. A visit to your pediatrician.

2. Urinalysis.

3. A visit to the urologist if the pediatrician recommends it.

4. A consultation with a child psychiatrist to find out if other commonly associated psychiatric conditions exist and to diagnose any possible stressor that may have missed detection. Professional treatment will probably entail use of a nighttime alarm and/or possibly medication such as a tricyclic antidepressant (e.g., imipramine) or DDAVP nasal spray, which inhibits production of urine (the alarm–plus–imipramine combination has proven to be especially successful in many cases).

SEE ALSO

STRESS   PSYCHOTROPIC MEDICATION
SEXUAL ABUSE   AND CHILDREN
LANGUAGE DISORDERS   ALL TYPES OF THERAPY
LEARNING DISORDERS

CHAPTER THIRTY-TWO
Encopresis (Soiling)

*"Andy? What's this I just found under the bed? Your under-
wear is all dirty—why didn't you tell me this was here?
You're too old for this kind of nonsense!"*

Andy is six years old and he's just started second grade. His
mother's exasperation is understandable, since until now Andy
hadn't seemed to have any problem with toilet training—
after a bit of resistance, he learned to use the bathroom fairly
reliably by the age of three and hadn't had any significant accidents since. But now, in second grade, he seemed a bit
more anxious—and started once again pooping in his pants.
Andy was mortified, and his mother was baffled: Why was
he suddenly regressing to this infantile behavior?

There are two categories of encopresis—clinically defined
as the repetitive passing of feces in inappropriate places, the
most common inappropriate place being the child's underwear: (1) encopresis in children who have never gained control of their bowel movements, and (2) encopresis in children
who once were able to control their bowel movements but
have subsequently lost that control. Andy exhibits the second
of these categories.

Until the age of about four years, soiling accidents happen
to nearly all children. Thus the diagnosis of encopresis cannot
be made until after that time. In fact, many children continue
to have accidents past this age and still do not qualify for this
diagnosis until they reach the threshold of at least one soiling
episode per month, continuing for a period of three months.
Most children who soil themselves don't do it on purpose.
The great majority of children who have encopresis generally

have it because of excess fluid in their bowels—a condition deriving from stress, diarrhea, and/or constipation. Constipated children in particular may be "backed up" for as much as a week at a time, eventually—and painfully—passing the solid fecal mass, only to have the syndrome of retention begin again. During the period of constipation, there is often leakage of soft stool around the hard fecal mass, causing encopresis. Some children just have urgent bowel movements over which they have no control. Only a very small minority of children voluntarily pass feces inappropriately.

Not surprisingly, most children who have encopresis are ashamed of it. Like Andy, they often try to hide their underwear, and they often smell. At school they typically become objects of scorn to other children, who generally label them with some pretty nasty nicknames. Hiding their underwear often results in terrible odors in their rooms and the parent's discovery of the hidden underwear stuffed into the backs of closets, in dresser drawers, or under mattresses and beds. We don't know definitively what causes encopresis. Sometimes it is associated with physical abnormalities of the rectal sphincter or rectum itself; however, while these abnormalities may be the cause of encopresis, they may also be a symptom of sustained constipation as well. There also appears to be a strong connection to stress. Children who live under chronic stress are more likely to have encopresis. There have been several theories about possible causes of encopresis, ranging from conflicts with parents, severe bowel training during the toddler stage, and other family-derived difficulties (neglect, abuse, divorce, sibling rivalry, etc.). Children who have been abused or sexually molested or in other ways severely traumatized may have encopresis, as do some retarded children. It has been my experience that that many encopretic children are often quite oppositional and the encopresis appears as a passive-aggressive act, which is part of their resistance to authority (see the chapter on behavior disorders). However, to some degree this is as baffling as the chicken and the egg: What is cause and what is symptom have still not been determined.

WHAT TO DO

1. First of all, keep in mind that the odds are that whatever you do, the encopresis will clear up on its own as the child matures. Reflect for a moment that you rarely encounter an encopretic teenager or adult.

2. Despite the dramatic predicament this condition presents often to the whole family, parents should refrain from criticizing, disparaging, teasing, or in any way treating the child in a hurtful or punishing way. Remember that the one who is suffering the worst from this condition isn't you, it's your child. Causing your child further shame will only make him or her further and more negatively affected by the issues that caused the encopresis in the first place.

3. Certainly take your child to a pediatrician so that organic causes may be ruled out: bowel irregularities such as diseases of the colon, narrowing of the sphincter, an enlarged bowel, general disease of the muscular system, and in some rare cases hormonal abnormalities. Take note of the pattern of your child's encopresis so that you can report it to your pediatrician: Does it typically happen in the morning, afternoon, night, before or after a meal, when your child goes to school, on weekends? Is it related to family situations such as a recent move, divorce, or death? Also take note of your child's diet: Is it high enough in fiber from fruits, whole grains, and vegetables?

4. After your pediatrician has ruled out organic causes (as s/he more than likely will), your child will probably be put on a bowel-training program in which his/her bowels are emptied (a process called catharsis)

and then gently "retrained" as to when to go to the bathroom, as well as be given a diet richer in fiber (the fiber increase should be gradual, not dramatic). Often laxatives at very low doses are used, along with behavioral training such as putting your child on the toilet at regular intervals and, of course, offering positive reinforcement when bowel movements are made. A combination of improving the diet, retraining, and positive reinforcement generally proves most successful.

5. If these measures don't work, professional consultation is usually called for. A mental health-care professional may recommend other forms of therapy, including individual psychotherapy, family therapy, family group therapy, and sometimes even medication. Low doses of antidepressants along with bowel propulsive agents have sometimes proven successful.

SEE ALSO

BEHAVIOR DISORDERS

PSYCHOTROPIC MEDICATION
   AND CHILDREN

ALL TYPES OF THERAPY

ENURESIS (WETTING)

STRESS

SEXUAL ABUSE

CHILD PHYSICAL ABUSE

CHAPTER THIRTY-THREE

Psychosomatic Disorders

"But I can't help it, Mom—my head hurts! And I feel dizzy all the time. I'm sick, I just know I'm sick. So what if the doctor doesn't know what I have—doctors don't know everything!"

Nine-year-old Harry is right: Doctors don't know everything. But doctors—and child psychiatrists and other mental health care professionals—do often encounter what it turns out is really bothering Harry: what we call a conversion disorder, in which emotional stress is converted into bodily complaints. The pain Harry feels is real, and his parents have made sure that he's had a full medical workup to rule out any physical causes for that pain. At the suggestion of their medical doctor, they've consulted a child psychiatrist for guidance. He has pointed out that Harry's mother frequently complains of similar headaches and dizziness that have no discernible physical cause. It is likely, the child psychiatrist has suggested, that Harry has learned to deal with stress the covert way he has seen his mother deal with it: once again, converting it into bodily pain.

Psychosomatic disorders have a long history. For over a hundred years there have been many reports of patients with unexplainable physical symptoms. The umbrella diagnosis for such complaints was "hysteria"—the affliction Freud most frequently sought to cure when he started his own practice. Such psychosomatic pains were seen to be bodily expressions of underlying emotional issues—painful memories, unconscious conflicts, sometimes sexual abuse—that the complainant was unable to express in any other way.

We now call these emotionally based afflictions somato-form disorders, two major categories of which we see in young people. The first, the one Harry exhibits and by far the most common in preadolescents, is the aforementioned conversion disorder. Conversion symptoms—deficits in a child's sensory or motor functions that often resemble a physi-cal neurological or medical condition—are usually triggered by psychological conflicts or by stress. Most conversion dis-order symptoms occur during the school-age years and ap-pear to be slightly more common in girls than in boys. They usually happen in short-lived episodes and involve only one or two symptoms. Children frequently complain of weak-ness and sometimes even paralysis. Some children have trou-ble walking, talking, seeing, or hearing. They often complain of "funny feelings" or numbness in their hands or feet. In rarer cases, the child may actually not be able to get up off a seat or may have episodes of what appear to be full-blown seizures. Perhaps the most typical conversion reaction is pain. Although pain can develop anywhere in a child's body, it seems to occur most frequently in the abdominal area—a symptom so common that it is considered a separate syndrome in itself. Children who feel abdominal pain do, however, usually complain of other symptoms as well, most typically light-headedness, fainting, vague headaches, and a generalized feeling of being unwell, including nausea, vom-iting, and intestinal distress.

The second common type of somatoform disorder is called somatization disorder. This almost entirely affects adolescents—it is very rare in younger children. This disorder involves a pattern of chronic and multiple bodily complaints. In con-trast to conversion disorders, it is very long-lasting, tends to be recurrent, and has many symptoms.

It has been clear since the time of Freud that children with somatoform disorders—again, usually conversion disor-ders in the preadolescent years—suffer from emotional stress they cannot express or vent directly. This stress can result

from specific incidents, such as a death in the family, sexual
or physical abuse, living in a chaotic household, conflicts
with parents or siblings who themselves have many bodily
complaints, or from secret collusions with parents (e.g., a parent inappropriately confiding intimate details to the child).
Conversion symptoms can also persist after a real physical
malady, in which pain from, say, a broken arm continues to
be felt even after the arm has physically healed, or a child
who has had gastroenteritis continues to feel abdominal pain
long after the physical illness has subsided. The child has unconsciously seized on these "legitimate" pains to express
emotional conflict s/he feels s/he can express in no other way.

We are not quite sure why one child develops a somatoform
disorder and another doesn't, although there does seem to be a
possible genetic predisposition, and/or the child may learn the
behavior from parents who themselves exhibit a conversion
disorder (e.g., Harry and his mother). Trauma and abuse tend
to increase the likelihood of conversion disorders, and certain
children simply have more difficulty than others in expressing
their emotions directly, either because of their temperaments
or, sometimes, because of the felt constraints of whatever culture or subculture they may have been born into.

WHAT TO DO

1. Always remember that any child with physical symptoms may in fact be suffering from a real medical illness. It is important to go to your pediatrician to rule
   out any medical basis for your child's pain or bodily
   complaints. Up to 15 percent of children with recurrent abdominal pain actually do have something
   wrong with their gastrointestinal systems. Take your
   child's complaints seriously.

2. Become your pediatrician's ally. First of all, make sure
   you give him or her the child's complete medical his-

tory, and once the pediatrician has given your child a complete physical examination, if he/she suggests that the problem may be psychological, don't dismiss this possibility, as tempting as it may be to do so.

3. If physical causes of the child's bodily distress have been ruled out and the condition does not remit in a short period of time, it is probable that your pediatrician will give you a psychiatric referral. Psychotherapy is very helpful, particularly when it comes in the form of individual therapy combined with family therapy, the focus of both of which will be on (1) discovering what the child is trying to express through his or her bodily complaints and (2) helping the child not to avoid whatever these conflicts may be but rather express them verbally.

4. Try not to become upset or panicky when your child evinces psychosomatic pain. Your distress will often simply intensify your child's distress and reinforce adherence to his/her bodily symptoms.

5. Try to work with your child in figuring out what may be the triggers for somatic complaints. See if there have been any traumas the child has experienced that you may not know about or the impact of which you may have underestimated. You and your child can become co-diagnosticians in this process, and this will give your child a sense of control as well as strengthen a healthy bond between you.

6. Be a good role model for your child. Examine your own pattern of expressing distress, and if you see that you also tend to express emotional conflicts somatically, take measures—possibly through therapy—to alter this pattern.

7. Avoid extensive, recurrent, costly, and unnecessary medical tests. It is normal to feel anxious about your

child's pain, but if physical illness truly has been ruled
out by a responsible pediatrician, seeking additional
opinions will not help your child. Focus instead on
the possible psychological causes of his or her distress.

SEE ALSO

STRESS   ALL TYPES OF THERAPY
CHILD PHYSICAL ABUSE   ANXIETY
SEXUAL ABUSE

CHAPTER THIRTY-FOUR

The Physically Ill Child

"Come on, Mom, the weather's gonna be fine. Can't I go to the baseball game? Johnny's dad will be driving us. He'll be with us for the whole thing. He'll help me out of the car and everything. I feel okay—really I do. I'll be okay, honest! Can't I go? Please, Mom?"

For the chronically ill child—the child who may be battling anything from rheumatic fever or diabetes to muscular dystrophy or cancer—daily life can be a very stressful and demoralizing business. A chronic illness frightens and angers children. It sets them apart from their peers; they feel different, isolated, alienated. Activities are limited, opportunities for normal social interaction are curtailed, and the sick child may be terrified at his/her powerlessness over bodily functions and the prospect that the illness may prove fatal.

Typically, parents of physically ill children are anxious and angry themselves—sometimes feeling guilty for having "not done the right thing" for the child or even in some way for causing the illness themselves. They often overcompensate by seeking to shield or protect the child from any possible negative or dangerous influence, unwittingly increasing the child's own anxiety and feelings of isolation. (The little boy quoted above has parents like these.) At the other end of the spectrum, they may deny the seriousness of the illness and even shun or reject the child for being ill, usually out of the fear of facing their own feelings about the severity and threat of it.

Children's understanding of their own chronic illness varies according to their level of maturity. The younger and more immature the child is, the more he or she might be prone to see the illness as punishment for taboo thoughts, wishes, or behavior. The child may feel shame and even guilt for being ill. Most such children use the mechanism of feeling punished as a way of maintaining some sense of power over the illness: "If I hadn't been bad, I wouldn't be sick." Older children often displace their deep anxiety about their well-being and lack of control onto various procedures and other concrete aspects of the illness, becoming absorbed in the minutiae of their medicines and treatments, with a sometimes encyclopedic grasp of the most arcane medical details. This is also a way to subsume or vent their anxiety about new treatments and operations to which they may be subject, the prospects of which really cause them tremendous fear and anxiety.

WHAT TO DO

1. Be sure that you never lose sight of the fact that your child has an illness and that the illness does not have your child. In other words, keep in the forefront of your mind that your child is a whole person who happens to have an illness, and that there are many aspects of his or her body and mind that are healthy and normal. Remind the child of—and encourage the child to enjoy—the normal aspects of life to which he or she has access.

2. Your main job is not only to coordinate your child's physical treatment with his or her medical team, but to listen to your child's grief about having contracted a chronic illness. Allow your child to ventilate and express feelings—to give voice to the complete spectrum of reactions to the illness—while you remain calm. This is asking a lot of any parent, but it will also give something immeasurably valuable to your child.

3. Do not overprotect or overindulge your child, because it will limit positive activities in other areas that will help to boost his/her spirits.

4. Be sure to explain your child's illness to him or her in terms he or she can understand. Don't give more detail than the child can register, but also don't lie about aspects of the illness the child can comprehend. As always, be calm, direct, and as reassuring as possible when giving any information about the illness.

5. Keep your child as involved as possible in activities appropriate to his or her age, gender, and abilities. Art, music, videos, allowing him or her to go to a sports event under supervision, keeping him or her in contact with other children—all of these activities will help your child to feel less abnormal and more connected to the rest of the world.

6. You will have many feelings about your child's illness, ranging from anger and guilt to fear and doubt and anxiety. It is important to allow these feelings to come to consciousness so that you don't block them out and thus prevent yourself from responding as fully as you can to your child's own needs. Make use of any support groups or therapy options to which you have access (often in hospitals and medical centers; you can find out about them from your child's medical support team). Discuss your feelings with other family members. Try to avoid blaming others for your child's illness (such as your spouse, other children, a negligent teacher, or doctor or nurse); your energies are far more productively channeled into maintaining as positive a frame of mind as you can. Children look to parents for hope and truth, and indeed, there is no one in a child's life who can provide that yearned-for support better than a parent. Acknowledge and deal

with your own stress and grief; then communicate with your child in the most positive and loving manner you can.

SEE ALSO

ANGER   **STRESS**
ANXIETY

CHAPTER THIRTY-FIVE

Tics (Including Tourette's Syndrome)

"It's so embarrassing, Doctor. Ronnie will suddenly start twitching his eyes and face and sometimes let out a string of four-letter words. My sister thinks he may need to be institutionalized! What's wrong with him? Is he very disturbed?"

Tics—sudden, rapid, repetitive, but usually arrhythmic movements or gestures, and sometimes words or sounds—are disturbing both to the children they afflict and to the people around them. They are commonly misunderstood and regarded (wrongly) as evidence of mental illness or even psychosis. Until recently, even many therapists and health-care practitioners shared this view, and the unfortunate child who displayed tics was made to feel as if s/he were mentally retarded or emotionally disturbed. Recent studies indicate that tics are actually involuntary (although often repressible) phenomena whose cause is far more likely physical and/or genetic than psychological. However, as with other involuntary afflictions (such as stuttering), the secondary emotional problems for the tic sufferer can be considerable and debilitating. It's no fun to be out of control in this way in front of your friends, classmates, family, and teachers. It's frightening and confusing, and it often leads to severe social isolation and very low self-esteem.

Tics can take a wide variety of forms. Motor tics range from rapidly blinking eyes, head jerking, and shoulder shrugging to abdominal flexion, tongue thrusting, bizarre facial expressions, obscene gestures (copropraxia), and gesturing with hands, arms, and legs. Vocal tics can vary from simple repetitive throat clearing, sniffing, and coughing to blurting out words and phrases and shouting obscenities (coprolalia). There are three general categories of tic presentation: transient tic disorder, which goes away in a year or less; chronic tic disorder, which usually involves a combination of motor tics that start in the head and then move downward in the body (vocal tics may also be involved but rarely appear alone) and which lasts for longer than a year; and complex syndromes such as Tourette's syndrome, which enlarge into a vast variety of motor tics and, after several years, phonic or vocal tics, often including coprolalia and copropraxia, and sometimes manifesting in mimicry of other people, either vocally (echolalia) or gesturally (echopraxia).

Children who suffer from tics also suffer from the fear and misunderstanding and cruelty of other people—not just other kids, but sometimes family members and teachers as well. The family's frustration and anxiety just increase the child's dislike of him- or herself. The addition of obsessive-compulsive disorder, which is common in children with Tourette's syndrome, just worsens the picture for everybody. On the whole, children with tics seem to be more impulsive, hyperactive, and distractible than other children. Boys seem to suffer more from tics than girls.

Tics have been studied in great detail because of their dramatic nature and the ease with which they are diagnosed. As mentioned, it is now known that tics have a largely genetic basis. Family members of affected children have much higher rates of tic disorders than relatives of children who do not suffer from them. While the actual mechanism of the tic is not known, it is largely assumed that it has to do with particular neurotransmitters, especially dopamine, and their interaction with nervous system tissue. Hormones—especially testosterone and androgen (male hormones)—have often been associated with this dysfunction in children as well. The area of the brain seemingly most affected in children with tics is called the basal ganglia, which are deep brain structures involved in movement, among other functions.

While we now know that tics are not symptoms of neurosis (as they were once thought to be), they do seem to be exacerbated by stress. The good news about tics is that nearly all children who suffer from them—70 to 90 percent—no longer have them by the end of adolescence. The reason for this is not clear, but it may have something to do with the maturation of the nervous system as the child enters and progresses through the teenage years.

WHAT TO DO

1. If your child develops what appear to be involuntary movements you feel might be tics, consult your pediatrician to rule out any other neurological movement disorders.

2. Whatever the nature of the tics or tic syndromes from which your child may suffer, it is essential that you focus on the other areas of the child's life and not contribute to any sense of his or her being a pariah. Remember that tics very likely have a genetic and/or neurological basis and that your child is struggling with something over which he or she has very little control. They commonly are emotionally and intellectually exactly like other children and should not be treated as if they were seriously disturbed.

3. Children who develop a chronic tic disorder especially need to be assured that they are not emotionally or mentally abnormal, and certainly should not be disciplined into "snapping out" of their disorder. This may be difficult for parents who themselves suffered from tics as children in a far less enlightened era, when perhaps they were told that the tics were their

fault, evidence of weakness, perversity, or even insanity. Support, compassion, and patience will help secondary difficulties—such as obsessive-compulsive symptoms and attentional difficulties in school, as well as decreased self-esteem and social isolation—from taking over the child's life.

4. Children suffering from transient tics will benefit from stress reduction the most; parents should do all they can to identify what the worst stressors are in the child's life, and work to ease their impact.

5. The use of certain medications has been found to be extremely effective in children with Tourette's syndrome and sometimes also in those with chronic motor tics. Specifically, Haldol and pimozide have resulted in remission of tics in a short period of time in 70 to 80 percent of afflicted children. Another medication, clonidine, has helped up to a quarter of children who have these syndromes without the occasional neurological side effects of Haldol and pimozide, although with some of the same sedative side effects.

6. Children with chronic tic disorders and Tourette's syndrome usually need therapy, which focuses on the secondary and co-morbid problems they almost always have: loss of self-esteem, depression, and social isolation, as well as attentional, obsessive-compulsive, and learning difficulties. Family therapy is also very helpful not only for the education and support it can provide parents as well as the child, but also to deal with the conflicts that ensue from the impact of the child's disorder on home life.

7. Most important is to try to do everything you can not to damage your child emotionally or in any other way—and to remember that in every likelihood his or her affliction will pass by late adolescence.

SEE ALSO

ATTENTION DEFICIT DISORDER

OBSESSIVE-COMPULSIVE
   DISORDER

DEPRESSION AND MANIA

ALL TYPES OF THERAPY

PSYCHOTROPIC MEDICATION
   AND CHILDREN

THE UNDERACHIEVER

STRESS

LEARNING DISORDERS

CHAPTER THIRTY-SIX

Eating Disorders

"Randy! Get your head out of the refrigerator! You're nine years old and you weigh as much as I do! What? No, it's not baby fat, and it won't just come off by itself!"

Randy's mother wasn't always this blunt with him about his obesity. She says she's tried to be supportive and reassuring and give him nutritious low-fat meals ever since he started to put on excess weight a few years ago, but it's been a losing battle. Randy sneaks food out of the refrigerator, spends his allowance on candy and potato chips, and keeps gaining weight. In the United States, one in ten children shares his dilemma of being overweight, and many of their parents feel as frustrated as Randy's mother does—often because they themselves have battled obesity throughout their lives and want to spare their children the same fate. It's no fun to go through childhood with a nickname like Fatso.

Obesity is diagnosed in children if the child weighs at least one-fifth more than the appropriate weight for his or her age and height. Although many people blame obesity on hormone problems, it far more usually proceeds from an obvious cause: eating too much. Obesity seems to run in families, and while there may be some genetic predisposition for it, it is also commonly influenced by family problems. Children who are anxious or angry and/or who experience chaotic or disorganized home lives often become obese, especially if other family members are obese. Overeating is often one way to quell inner sensations of irritability, rage, depression, and other forms of distress. Obesity also tends to run in poorer families. As with many other psychiatric symptoms, being overweight usually causes secondary emotional problems: It lowers self-esteem, making depression and social isolation more likely. Medical complications from obesity include diabetes, elevated cholesterol, sleep problems, and general problems adjusting socially and in school. Treating obesity almost always requires investigating family dysfunction as well as working out an eating program that the child can be persuaded to follow. In particular, parents need to see that they are providing good models for sensible eating and/or not criticizing the child too harshly for overeating—which often just increases the temptation for the child to "escape" by reaching for more food.

The flip side of obesity is anorexia, which until recently wouldn't have warranted mention in a book about preadolescent children. Indeed, anorexia (deliberately depriving oneself of food) is still very much more common in adolescents than in preteens. However, because of the culture and media's emphasis on being thin—particularly for girls—there are increasing reports of it in prepubescent children, and thus it deserves inclusion here. Typically there is no weight loss in this group, but rather a failure to gain expected weight, slowing of growth, and delayed sexual development. As with older anorexics, the motive for undereating is an intense and irrational fear of getting fat, a fear that is often passed on to daughters by mothers who are themselves borderline anorexics.

In general, however, apart from obesity—which itself affects only one child in ten in this country—eating disorders tend to be far more common in adults than in children. The following disorders are particularly rare, but they are so severe that if your child should be one of the few afflicted by one or another of them, help should be sought immediately. As with obesity and anorexia, children who have an eating disorder usually have some difficulty in their relationship with caretakers; attachment disorders, in particular, are often implicated in an eating disorder. This means that treating the disorder almost always requires treating a larger family dysfunction.

Pica—defined officially as the persistent eating of non-nutritive substances—is an eating disorder that has drawn national attention because of children who have gotten lead poisoning from eating paint chips. However, children with pica eat many things other than paint—for example, pieces of clothing, dirt, feces, hair, wood, paper, and straw. Not surprisingly, there are many medical complications from this disorder, ranging from heavy metal poisoning and mineral/vitamin deficiencies to parasitic infections and sometimes obstruction of the intestines. It seems clear that lack of supervision—the product of a general neglect of the child—is the core cause for pica. The child experiences deprivation in nearly every part of life, emotional as well as nutritive—a neglect that often comes from parents with severe mental illness. Pica may also be part of another psychiatric syndrome, such as mental retardation, autism, or childhood schizophrenia.

Failure-to-thrive syndrome, which unfortunately is found in a sizable percentage of children admitted to hospitals for medical reasons, is characterized by a deceleration of weight gain, physical growth and height, and head circumference, accompanied by a similar slowing or disruption of social and emotional development. The physical deterioration is caused by decreased caloric intake, but the depression, social withdrawal, and apathy associated with this syndrome, as well as markedly negative family influences, conspire to intensify the syndrome, creating a vicious cycle that can be broken only by a dramatic improvement in the child's environment. As with pica, it most often occurs at a very young age—usually before the child is three years old. Because their immune systems are frequently impaired, children with this syndrome often become sick, and by the time the child reaches a pediatrician or the hospital it is sometimes hard to sort out what is the product of environmental influences and what is purely physical illness. However, the environmental influence is nearly always paramount, and this syndrome is frequently associated with physical abuse and medical and educational neglect. Indeed, failure to thrive is one of the more common reasons that children are removed from their homes and placed in foster care.

Rumination disorder, which involves regurgitating food and rechewing it, is rarer than failure-to-thrive syndrome, but its cause similarly seems to be rooted in a disordered attachment with the child's caretakers, as well as a response to deprivation. Some believe that regurgitating and rechewing food provides the child a way to turn inward and escape a painful or intolerable environment. As with pica and failure to thrive, it occurs most commonly in very young children (up to three years old). Medical complications of rumination disorder include lung infections due to breathing in regurgitated food (called aspiration) as well as malnutrition, growth failure, and developmental delays, and it sometimes even proves fatal. There can also be a relationship between this disorder and other physical problems, such as hiatal hernias and gastroesophageal reflux disorder.

Another rare syndrome that has as part of its definition an eating disorder is psychosexual dwarfism, which occurs in children between two and four years old and involves a deceleration of linear growth (although, unlike failure-to-thrive syndrome, no deceleration in weight gain) as well as a sleep disorder. The eating disorder can be quite bizarre, with problems ranging from overeating, gorging, stealing food, and hoarding food to vomiting, pica, drinking too much, and/or sometimes drinking dishwater or water from the toilet. Children with psychosocial dwarfism are usually aggressive and have behavior disorders as well as problems with intelligence. As with the other eating disorders, these children typically have difficulties bonding with caretakers and have suffered neglectful maltreatment. Happily, the syndrome is considered somewhat reversible if the environment is improved and the child receives the needed care and attention.

WHAT TO DO

1. If your child is obese, schedule a diagnostic consultation with your pediatrician. You should be sure to aim for a healthy diet with a total caloric intake appropriate to the child's age and height. Strict dieting is usually not indicated unless the obesity is so overwhelmingly severe that the child's life is threatened (and this is very rare). The diet should be balanced and interesting—take advantage of the many low-calorie diet and recipe books now available to make it as palatable as possible to your child.

2. As with every eating disorder, you need to be sensitive to any family dysfunction that may be contributing to your child's overeating, especially the model you are presenting to your child in your own eating habits. If you are battling obesity too, you may want to join forces with your child and make the hoped-for weight loss a true family affair. Focus also on any possible neglect your child may be experiencing, as well as on his or her anger, anxiety, and feelings of instability. Family therapy may be indicated.

3. If your child appears to be heading toward anorexia, have him or her checked for any medical problems by your pediatrician to rule out any physical contributing causes; then, as with obesity, make sure that your child is taking in an adequate number of calories from healthy foods, and examine what family dysfunction may be influencing your child's resistance to eating.

Change your own patterns, if necessary, to provide a healthier model for your child.

4. If you fear your child may have any of the rarer but quite serious eating disorders covered here—pica, failure-to-thrive syndrome, rumination syndrome, or psychosocial dwarfism—heed the fact that the core cause for each of them is neglect, a non-nurturing home life, and other forms of family dysfunction. The child's environment must change dramatically for there to be improvement in his or her eating habits and health. This will probably entail making significant changes in your own treatment of your child and the degree to which you offer your child the attention and care he or she needs. Family therapy is probably indicated.

- If you think your child has pica, you must have him or her see a doctor immediately, not only to rule out any psychiatric syndromes but to be sure that no medical complications are present. It is crucial that your child have a blood test to determine if lead poisoning (which can cause neurological symptoms, intestinal problems, anemia, decreased intelligence, constipation, and abnormally short height, and can lead to learning disorders and mental retardation) has occurred. This is treatable by iron supplements if it is not too severe, and by certain other medications if it is severe.

- If you fear your child may have failure-to-thrive syndrome—if your child's weight gain diminishes, if s/he is not reaching his or her milestones or growing as expected—immediate pediatric consultation is necessary. There is a growing number of specialists in this area who will be able to do the complex evaluation it will take to make this diagnosis.

- If your child has rumination disorder, you must see a pediatrician to rule out any medical causes and to examine the child for evidence of any of the afore-mentioned medical complications.

- If you feel your child may have psychosexual dwarfism, once again a pediatric consultation is necessary to rule out contributing medical causes, particularly (in the case of this syndrome) hormonal difficulties and problems with the pituitary gland as well as other congenital syndromes.

SEE ALSO

PERVASIVE DEVELOPMENTAL
DISORDER (AUTISM)
SCHIZOPHRENIA
DEPRESSION AND MANIA
ALL TYPES OF THERAPY
CHILD PHYSICAL ABUSE

PSYCHOSOMATIC DISORDERS
ATTACHMENT DISORDERS
ANGER
SLEEP DISORDERS
BEHAVIOR DISORDERS
ANXIETY

SEXUALITY

Chapter Thirty-seven
Sexual Development

"Jimmy is only two and when I give him a bath, he—well, he gets aroused! Am I doing something bad, or is there something wrong with him? Isn't he too young to be sexual?"

We are sexual beings from the time we are born to the day we die. This is a distressing notion to a lot of parents, whose own ambivalent feelings about sex and sexuality make them uncomfortable with the notion that their children, even in infancy and toddlerhood, have sexual feelings and indulge in sexual play. Even in the womb, the fetus can be seen to touch his or her body and genitals. Sucking, biting, caressing, fondling, playing with one's own genitals and/or anus, curiosity about bowel habits, becoming erotically stimulated by breast-feeding and (as in Jimmy's case) getting a bath—all these are perfectly normal manifestations of a child's sexuality. Erotic attachments to the mother or father may occur in children as young as one and a half. Girls of two may express the desire to have a penis, boys of the same age may wish they had breasts, and "playing doctor" is an almost universal experience for children throughout early and middle childhood. In fact, between the ages of three and about five and a half most children participate in a whole range of erotic play: curiosity about other people undressing, displaying genitals at home and sometimes in public, masturbation, and even inserting objects into the vagina and rectum. The famed "Oedipus complex"—in which the child by the age of four or five conceives a powerful desire for the parent of the opposite sex—is more evidence of normal childhood sexual

development. From age five up to adolescence, sexual thoughts
and play may appear to disappear or go underground—which
is why Freud called this the latency period—but in fact they're
still evident in the many sexually oriented jokes, pictures,
and games children play and share with each other. The bot-
tom line is that erotic curiosity and sexual exploration in
children are completely healthy, and while it may be unnerving for parents to discover evidence of it in their children,
there is generally no need to worry about it.

Indeed, the most common problems parents and children
face regarding sex have to do with the mixed messages and
feelings about sex that we all get from the culture and from
our own families. As with so many difficulties the child faces
at home, it is often the parents' reactions to those difficulties
that worsen or intensify the problem. One mother who considered herself very liberal in sexual matters consulted me
because she was disturbed by the behavior of her young son,
whom she had caught masturbating after she had permis-
sively allowed him to view a sexually provocative adult film
on video. She missed the fact that she herself had provided
him with the stimulation to masturbate, and blamed her son
entirely for poor self-control. This contradictory mixture of
puritanism and prurience characterizes much of American
society's general sexual confusion, and probably none of us
escapes the dilemma, particularly when we're faced with
dealing with our children about sex.

Because parents' feelings and thoughts about sex are often
so charged and ambivalent, and because of the cultural mixed
messages all of us (including children) get about sex, there is
no easy route through this thorny passage. Perhaps in no
other area of the parent-child relationship do we more need
to take our time before we respond to the sexual questions,
curiosity, and behavior of our children. We need to be flexible and act on a case-by-case basis, trying as assiduously as
we can to keep our own reflexive judgments at bay so that

we can allow ourselves to "get the big picture." This realm is especially difficult because for so many families the issue of sex is a highly moral one. A child who misbehaves sexually is sometimes very quickly labeled "bad" or even "evil"; this is a damning conclusion that can scar a child quite badly. Children who are induced to feel too much shame about their sexual thoughts and feelings are generally the ones headed for a wide spectrum of trouble, sexual and otherwise. Compassion, restraint, and a sense of humor go a long way toward helping children navigate these confusing and uncomfortable straits. However, it's not only harsh, anxious, and punitive parents who cause significant distress about sex in their kids. Parents who completely neglect or ignore the problem may also unwittingly encourage a damaging, unhelpful, and overly secretive approach to sex in their children. Even very bright or intellectually gifted parents who converse with their children about every topic under the sun sometimes clam up when it comes to sex, giving the unwelcome message that this topic is shameful and off-limits.

Some degree of distress in this realm is probably inevitable. None of us deals perfectly with our children about sex, and certainly by the latency stage, most children have adopted the same outward modesty about sex that they see in their own families. Although the preschooler has exciting and vivid sexual thoughts and images as well as an intense curiosity about intercourse, where babies come from, and other sexual matters, by the time children reach school age they generally demonstrate the same sexual restraint they see in their families and communities. Sexual knowledge is typically gained on the sly—sneaking into libraries to look up "the good parts" of books; poring in secret over medical volumes, pornography, or adult sex guides; and especially getting information from peers, which often gives children some pretty distorted ideas about anatomy, what goes where, and what sex is all about. However, by the middle-school years and certainly by adolescence, most children are secure in their gender identity (girls know they are girls, boys know they are boys) and have sorted out sexual fact from fiction.

Again, problems usually come more from contradictory emotional, family, and cultural messages about sex rather than from knowledge or lack of knowledge of sexual mechanics. But parents can do much to ease this confusion. Perhaps most important is to review one's own childhood anxieties and questions about sex and cultivate as much patience and compassion for our own children's sexual feelings and curiosities as we can. That stance will help us to deal even with our children's most perplexing questions about sex in the healthiest possible ways.

WHAT TO DO

1. Parents frequently express concern about whether it is harmful for their children to see them naked. In general, it is wise for parents not to appear nude before their children. Even if children appear to be handling it in stride, it still is overstimulating, and thus can interfere with a child's sexual development. The idea of "private parts" is an important concept to the growing child, because it is part of learning to differentiate oneself from parents—more evidence that "this is me" and "that is you." However, should such exposure happen accidentally, it is equally important that parents not make too much of it or react with shame, panic, or too much anxiety. We teach our children probably far more powerfully by example than by what we say. Making sure we do not communicate acute embarrassment or shame about sex or accidental nudity to our children, and calmly answering any questions they may have about their or our bodies, constitutes the best way of ensuring that they don't develop distorted perspectives about sexuality.

2. Answer all of your child's questions about sex, but in a way appropriate to his/her age and sexual development. You don't need to give a child more information than he or she is able to process, but if your child is able to frame a specific question, then he or she is able to register and process a simple and direct answer to that question. Do not use slang names for body parts; use the proper terms. But above all, adopt a matter-of-fact, compassionate, and commonsense tone. Your child learns as much from your own emotional approach to sex as he or she will from any technical facts you offer.

3. The flirtatiousness we commonly see in children at the oedipal age of four or five—in which the boy commonly acts seductively with his mother, and the girl does so with her father—is generally not as dramatic as Freud made it sound, but should it arise, there is no reason to worry about it. It is temporary, and marks an important stage of gender identity development.

4. Sexual development can be seen to be problematic in the case of the following:

   a. If a child shows no curiosity about sex (which indicates that there has been an alteration in the loving parent-child relationship).

   b. If the child exhibits excessive or precocious sexual behavior, such as asking to engage in sex, imitating adult sexual activity to an extreme, asking to perform or receive oral sex, or compulsively and repetitively inserting objects into the vagina or anus. This may indicate that the child has been sexually abused.

   c. If a child persistently acts like the opposite gender or complains about discomfort with being the gender that he/she is, it is possible that gender identity disorder is present.

SEE ALSO

MASTURBATION   SEXUAL ABUSE

GENDER IDENTITY DISORDER

CHAPTER THIRTY-EIGHT
Masturbation

"I've read that masturbation is supposed to be normal, but yesterday I caught Linda playing with herself—and she's only four! Where did she learn to do this? Isn't this unhealthy in such a little girl?"

Masturbation—the manipulation of genitals to produce sexual pleasure—is probably a universal human sexual act. People do it for a simple reason: It feels good. However, despite the frequently repeated news that masturbation is not physically or emotionally unhealthy, parents still often react in horror at the discovery that their children "play with themselves," especially if they discover such play in very young children. They believe—wrongly—that sex is something that only happens to you at puberty.

As you've seen in our discussion of sexual development, children are sexual from the time they are born—if not before, in the womb. Children's physical self-explorations, and masturbation in particular, mark important milestones: They allow children a sense of mastery over their feelings and bodies. Emotional problems associated with masturbation far more frequently arise from anxious parental reactions to it than from the act itself.

Many widely held misconceptions persist—for example, that girls (because they lack penises) don't masturbate; that it is abnormal for preadolescent children, boys or girls, to masturbate; that masturbation drains physical and intellectual energy; and/or that it means the child is pathologically "oversexed" or antisocial. None of these is true. And as for little Linda being "too young," parents need to remember that children between the ages of three and five are in many ways the most intensely sexual they will be in their lives; their curiosity about penises and breasts and vaginas is at an all-time high. They love to run around naked and often want others to be naked with them. They play doctor. They may engage not only in private but mutual masturbatory play with other children. By the time they enter school, children generally feel a fierce conflict between their sexual curiosities and desires and the internalized modesty and conscience they have derived from their families and culture. Overt sexual play—including masturbation—generally decreases, and may even seem to disappear. However, we should not conclude that children become any less sexual than they were before (or will be later); they may simply have learned to be more covert about their feelings and fantasies and behavior. They probably still masturbate, but they do so in private.

WHAT TO DO

1. Once parents understand that masturbation is normal, is life-enhancing, and encourages healthy development, they will realize that nothing really needs to be done about it. The one gentle admonition it's a good idea to pass on is simply this: Ask that your child do it in private.

2. Correlatively, reacting harshly or vehemently to public masturbation is counterproductive. It induces unreasonable guilt and shame, erodes the child's self-esteem, and promotes fearful attitudes about sex. Simply tell the child that public masturbation is inappropriate.

3. Masturbation is a problem when it is excessive, which is to say when it takes the place of other family, educational, social, or cultural activities in which the child is expected to participate. Children who won't stop masturbating, whether in public or private, are

using the behavior to give vent to underlying anxieties. The parent's task is to find out what those anxieties may be. Family conflicts, parental anxiety, and sometimes sexual abuse may be at the root of this excess. Talk to the child and, if necessary, have the child engage in private or family therapy if the causative anxiety is not readily apparent.

SEE ALSO

SEXUAL DEVELOPMENT   SEXUAL ABUSE
ANXIETY

CHAPTER THIRTY-NINE

Gender Identity
Disorder

"Benjamin, if I catch you wearing my slip one more time . . ."

The recognition that one is male or female constitutes one of the most fundamental components of identity—of knowing who one is. By the age of two, boys generally know they are male, girls that they are female. This does not mean that every child secure in this knowledge displays the same masculine or feminine traits. Some boys would rather read or even play with dolls than roughhouse or play football; some girls are more comfortable on a baseball diamond than in a ballet class. This also does not mean that boys and girls don't sometimes wonder what it might be like to be (or have the traits of) the other sex. Penis and breast envy (or at least curiosity about what it would be like to have them) are not some perverse psychoanalyst's invention. Many perfectly normal children fantasize in this way; it's part of the normal inquiry of the human imagination. However, even during these fantasy investigations, the acknowledgment and acceptance of one's own gender is generally not in question. Whatever their individual personalities or predilections, most boys know they are boys; most girls know they are girls.

Some children—whom we diagnose with gender identity disorder—feel far less sure about this. Some boys and girls simply feel that they were born into the wrong bodies. They exhibit what is called gender dysphoria: acute discomfort with being the gender they are. A boy with gender identity disorder usually exhibits a strong preference for toys, games, attitudes, clothing, and behavior culturally associated with girls, such as playing house, learning to cook, applying makeup and jewelry, and wearing a dress. He may appear effeminate from a very early age—sometimes as early as two or three. He may physically attempt to "lose" his penis, pushing it down between his legs so that it disappears and is more like female genitalia; he may sit down to urinate. He will probably seek out the company of girls, with whom he identifies far more strongly than with other boys. Similarly, girls with this disorder are usually far more than "tomboys": They quite explicitly long for a penis, may stand up to urinate, may lower their voices, long for crew cuts, engage in rough-and-tumble "masculine" games such as wrestling and football, have sports heroes as role models, and in other ways make it clear that they'd rather be male than female.

Because gender identity is so fundamental to most people—and normally so unquestioned in our society—boys and girls with gender identity disorder (GID) have a particularly rough time of it. By the latency period, when boys bond with boys, girls with girls, children with GID are typically—and mercilessly—shunned and made fun of by other kids. However, the worst criticism may come from parents. A boy who wants to be a girl is often particularly threatening to a father; similarly, a girl uncomfortable with being female will usually alienate her mother. It is probably true that every parent in some way lives through his or her child; we expect to some degree to see ourselves reflected in our sons and daughters, nowhere more than with regard to gender. Less consciously, parents' hidden fears and insecurities about their own masculinity and femininity can be very painfully stoked by an effeminate son or a masculine daughter. As a result, it isn't only schoolmates who lash out at children with GID; some of the most painful rejection is experienced at home from the family.

It is not known what causes gender identity disorder. There have been recent provocative and interesting studies about genetics and possible hormonal imbalances in utero. Birth order and physical appearance may have some contributory role. Parental desire for a boy or a girl may also have an impact: The child may sense that he or she was not born the "right" sex and unconsciously strives to become what he or she perceives is the gender the parents really wanted. Parent-child conflicts, overbearing maternal or paternal influence, and various other pathologies exhibited by parents may also have an impact. But nothing has been proven as the definitive cause.

It must be remembered that not every boy and girl who doesn't exhibit the "right" cultural or family styles of masculinity and femininity has GID. Gender identity disorder is a profound, entrenched, and very rare condition. The child with GID will more than likely be marked by it for life— sometimes investigating and pursuing a sex-change operation. It should also be noted that in many major cities there are support groups for men and women who regard themselves as "transgender" and do not see this condition necessarily as pathology.

WHAT TO DO

1. Remember that not every "sissy" or "tomboy" has GID. If your child doesn't exhibit conventional gender traits, it may simply be his or her style and personality. Be supportive, not punitive. Understand that he or she is probably already having a hard time at school for not appearing to be a "real" boy or girl. These children need love and understanding at home.

2. If your child identifies very strongly with the other sex, it is important to get professional help—the earlier the better.

3. Family, group, and individual psychotherapy are all very helpful. The goals of such treatments are to ad-

dress underlying problems and to decrease feelings of stigmatization and isolation, and possibly to prevent the GID from taking root. Parents do need to realize that they may have to change certain expectations about their child's development and that their child's happiness may depend upon the parents' acceptance of certain traits and lifestyle choices for which they may not have wished but which nonetheless promise the most positive outcome for the child.

SEE ALSO

Sexual Development

CHAPTER FORTY

Sexual Abuse

"Please, Mommy, I don't want Aunt Lillian and Uncle Jack to baby-sit. They make me play funny games I don't like. Please don't leave me with them. . . ."

According to state child abuse registries, sexual abuse—the exploitation of a child by an adult to satisfy the adult's sexual desires—accounts for 10 percent of all reported cases of child abuse. The operative word is *reported*. In fact, the actual incidence of sexual abuse of children may be as high as 20, 25, even 30 percent if we believe the many uncontrolled anecdotal studies reported so frequently in the media and professional journals. Many children don't disclose the abuse; adults similarly hide their own participation in it. Indeed, we know that the incidence is much higher than 10 percent from the number of adults—predominantly women—who reveal in adulthood that they were sexually abused in childhood (as many as 20 to 40 percent of adult women and 10 percent of men admit to having experienced some form of sexual tampering). Forms of sexual abuse also vary widely, including modes in which there may be only visual or verbal but no physical contact (e.g., the adult stares at an undressed child, walks naked in front of the child, or makes sexually provocative statements to the child); petting and fondling; masturbating in front of the child or masturbating the child him/herself; and genital/oral, genital/anal, and genital/genital contact. Perhaps most unnerving is that two-thirds of reported cases take place within the family, which means that the most common mode of sexual abuse is incest. Children may be sexually exploited by parents, stepparents, grandparents, aunts, uncles, and older siblings as well as by people from outside the family, such as neighbors, teachers, and baby-sitters.

Forty percent of children who are abused experience it only once in their lives, but an appalling 60 percent experience it many more times, often over a period of years. Both boys and girls, from infancy to adolescence, may be abused, although girls appear to be the more usual victims—some reliable study statistics indicate that as many as one in every six girls is sexually exploited by an adult.

These are disturbing figures, enough to make parents and family members justifiably nervous and concerned about any child's welfare. In fact, the problem may be even more delicate and difficult. If you are consulting this chapter, it may be because you have been the perpetrator of this abuse and want to stop, or suspect that another family member, friend, neighbor, relative, or baby-sitter has victimized your child. But even if you are only distressed generally about the possibility of sexual abuse, you already know that this whole realm is full of shame and secrecy. There is no harm worse or more forbidding in many parents' minds than the possibility that their children have been or might one day be sexually exploited by an adult.

Sexual abuse in children is even harder to diagnose while it is happening, because fully 25 to 35 percent of victimized children show no symptoms of the abuse. However, two-thirds do develop symptoms, which may range from anxiety, dissociation, depression, or expressions of anger to a general decline in social, academic, and overall functioning. Studies of children who have been sexually abused indicate that 60 to 70 percent develop a psychiatric disorder—most commonly post-traumatic stress disorder, but also various behavior, anxiety, depressive, and dissociative disorders. Dissociative disturbances may include avoiding people, numbness, daydreaming, obsessive fantasizing, depersonalization (objectifying oneself or others), and such somatic complaints as fainting and feelings of physical helplessness. Children suffering from post-

traumatic stress disorder as a result of sexual abuse become
highly anxious, often reexperiencing the trauma in flashbacks,
and sometimes reenacting the trauma through sexual acting
out. Such children frequently battle depression. Depressed children typically feel shame and guilt, as if they were themselves
responsible for bringing on the abuse. Sometimes this depression becomes suicidal: The child's core identity is so funda-
mentally disturbed that he or she feels hurt beyond repair.
Such children also commonly become enraged and quick to
act out violently. They frequently have a hard time interacting
with other people, whether adults, or friends and classmates
their own age.

Many children who are sexually abused act out sexually
in highly inappropriate ways with other adults they meet.
They often have confused ideas about sexuality, closeness,
and intimacy. They may masturbate obsessively, sometimes
in public; reach to touch other people's genitals; act out
sexual intercourse; or say sexually provocative things. Some
children develop gender identity problems; others become
sexually phobic. Certainly a child exhibiting symptoms of
post-traumatic stress disorder who also acts out sexually is
very likely a victim of sexual abuse.

Not every child experiences these severe reactions; it depends on the nature of the abuse and the temperament and
age of the child. However, clearly some very serious psychic
consequences can proceed from sexual abuse, and parents
need to take seriously any indications that it may be occurring now or has occurred in the past.

WHAT TO DO

1. The most important measure parents can employ
   against sexual abuse is to make sure it doesn't happen
   in the first place. Children need to be given a solid
   education about what is appropriate and inappropri-

ate physical contact, and especially should be taught not to allow anyone to touch their genitals or otherwise fondle them inappropriately. This information should not be given in a way that alarms the child, as if sexual abusers were lurking around every corner. However, certainly if the child is touched in an inappropriate way by anyone, s/he should be encouraged to report it to parents or teachers immediately.

2. If your child discloses to you that s/he has been abused, remain calm—do not make the child's disclosure further reason to feel shame or anxiety.

3. Children should be taught that they have the right to say "No!" or "Stop!" to anyone who touches them inappropriately, even adults. It is empowering for children to know that no one has the right to touch them in certain ways, no matter how grown-up, important, or authoritative that person may be.

4. If your child evinces any of the post-traumatic, dissociative, angry, or depressed reactions or symptoms mentioned above—especially open masturbation, sexually provocative language, or other forms of sexual acting out—do consider that sexual abuse may have occurred, and help the child to talk freely and openly about his or her feelings. Other signs may be unexplained periods of sadness, enuresis, genital infection, or any abrupt change in social or academic functioning. Very young children may be able to communicate with you about the abuse by acting it out with stuffed animals or dolls or through drawings. Help your child to vent whatever feelings, thoughts, or obsessions may be fueling his or her distress. It may be the only way you will be able to find out what has happened to her or him.

5. If you know that your child has been sexually abused, do not panic, but do realize that it is a crime. The police should be contacted. You should arrange for an

198

immediate physical and mental health evaluation for your child. Take immediate action, but without alarming your child unduly.

6. The mental health evaluation should be carried out by a counselor, social worker, doctor, nurse, psychologist, or psychiatrist who has specific experience with child sexual abuse.

7. Remember that even if your child is or has been sexually abused—even over a long period—this does not necessarily have to result in serious psychiatric problems. However, it is true that the sooner the abuse is discovered and appropriate therapy can be employed, the better the child's chances will be of healing from the trauma.

8. If you are the perpetrator of the abuse or if you realize that another family member has perpetrated the abuse, you need to make sure the offending behavior is halted immediately. This often means removing yourself or the offending family member from the home until adequate therapy has been effected. It is difficult to admit that our own behavior may be at fault, especially in the realm of sexual abuse, but because the potential harm to your child is so great, you need to take immediate measures to stop the abuse and, as appropriate, seek therapeutic help either for yourself or for whichever family member may be victimizing the child.

SEE ALSO

FAMILY

CHAPTER FORTY-ONE
Divorce

"Mommy, could Daddy come over for dinner on Saturday if I promise to be real good? I'll wash all the dishes and clean my room and everything!"

Sandra, seven years old, is typical of many children of divorced parents—her mother says she's constantly trying to bring her father back home, and while Sandra doesn't say that she thinks she's the reason they broke up, her constant promises to be good imply she does in fact think the divorce was at least partly her fault. "I don't understand it," Sandra's mother tells me. "I mean, it's not like divorce is such an uncommon thing anymore. Plenty of Sandra's schoolmates live in single-parent homes or have parents who've split up. It shouldn't be such a trauma anymore. But it is."

Sandra's mother is right. Despite the fact that 50 percent of American marriages end in divorce, the effects of divorce on both parents and children are as traumatic and negative as they have ever been. Children of divorced parents typically have trouble forging intimate relationships well into adulthood; their self-esteem may be damaged, and their capacity to love and trust is often curtailed by the experience of having lived through their parents' splitting up. Divorce is experienced as a traumatic event, with loss, pain, grief, and feelings of hopelessness and abandonment all assailing the child—often in addition to the feeling that, like Sandra, they have somehow caused the parting to happen. It is a phenomenon that should be taken far more seriously than the media (which often would have us see divorce as not that big a thing anymore) imply.

The divorce itself, of course, is only part of what causes the trauma. Few divorces are not preceded by many months and sometimes years of mounting distress and discontent. The child may have seen parents fight—sometimes becoming violent—many times before the actual breakup. Witnessing their parents' growing alienation from one another increases anxiety in children, even if they may not talk about it; younger children, especially, often feel guilt or responsibility for having caused the problem. Hearing their own names shouted out in arguments and being harshly criticized for any infraction and/or otherwise poorly treated by a parent misdirecting his or her anger at the child can cause children to feel rejected, morose, abandoned, guilty, and/or angry. Toddlers and preschoolers can be quite badly scarred, often showing developmental regression, in which recently acquired skills (especially motor and language skills) may diminish or be lost. Some throw tantrums or cry nonstop; others become withdrawn or overly clingy in their attachments. Older children often begin showing academic and behavioral difficulties at school. Nearly all children show signs of sadness, some even of depression. The period prior to divorce is particularly painful and crippling to children who have preexisting emotional problems. Added to this is the fact that the parents' own anxiety and self-absorption throughout the divorce period often keeps them from being there for their children just when their children most need their attention and care.

After a divorce, problems continue for most children. Changes in economic stability, missing a parent, possibly moving to a new school or neighborhood, losing old friends, the stress of making new friends, being asked to take sides (having their loyalty tested), becoming scapegoats, adjusting to their parents' new lovers or relationships, eventually adjusting to stepparents and stepsiblings—all of these are potentially traumatic to the child of divorced parents.

WHAT TO DO

1. Don't put children in the middle. Don't make them messengers between the two of you at any time prior to, during, or after the divorce.

2. Go out of your way to reassure your children that they have in no way caused your marital problems.

3. Try to keep relations cordial if not friendly with your partner, especially when your child is around.

4. If possible, tell your child about the separation and divorce together. Use simple, accurate, but not overly detailed language about the reasons for it. Be sure to sketch out in clear detail what the postdivorce situation will be for your child—where the child will live, what the arrangements are for seeing both parents, and any potential changes in the child's lifestyle—all in service of making it clear what the child can expect at every step of the way. This will decrease stress and anxiety for both parents and child.

5. Make sure your child stays connected to the noncustodial parent. This is often one of the hardest goals to achieve in a divorce because of the enmity and unresolved conflicts and hostilities each partner frequently feels about the other, but it's one of a parent's most important tasks.

6. Make sure that visits to the parent with whom the child is not living are respected and not used as occasions to find out what the other parent is doing or thinking. Once again, do not use your child as a messenger or a spy. The noncustodial parent should make sure that the child's experience during visits is as normal and close to familiar routine as possible.

7. Encourage your child to express feelings freely, and be prepared for a great deal of anger expressed toward both parents, but especially toward the parent who

has custody of the child. The absent parent is often idealized, and the one with whom the child lives is often devalued (devaluing this parent gives the child more sense of permission to express rage at him or her).

8. Point out, when possible, whatever constructive aspects there may be to life after the divorce: for example, that there are now fewer arguments and fights (or even less violence) at home, and there is an overall decrease in tension. Also point out the positive aspects of whatever new living situation (neighborhood, school, etc.) the child may now be in.

9. Remember that every constructive intervention you do at this time for your child will pay off in the prevention of major emotional difficulties later on. You may not always be able to see the positive effects of your actions, but you can be sure that they are helping and will help your child immeasurably in the years to come.

10. If your child develops what appear to be more serious signs of anxiety, depression, post-traumatic stress reaction, developmental regression, academic difficulties, and the like, be sure to get a mental health evaluation and have your child participate in appropriate therapy. Acquaint yourself with the many support groups for children of divorce at schools, local clubs, and other institutions; investigate as well the many support groups for parents going through divorce.

SEE ALSO

STRESS   ANGER
THE UNDERACHIEVER   GRIEF
DEPRESSION AND MANIA   SINGLE PARENTS

CHAPTER FORTY-TWO

Sibling Rivalry

"Why do I always get blamed for stuff? I didn't do it, Dad—Joey did! Just 'cause he's the youngest, he always gets away with everything."

Say "sibling" to the average person in a word association test, and very likely the response you'll get is "rivalry." In a sense, this is too bad. To have the first association be rivalry when we think about brothers and sisters gives an inaccurate picture of the mainly positive role siblings have in each other's lives. In fact, while there are reams of psychiatric literature addressed to parent-child dynamics, very little has been addressed to sibling relationships. This is striking given how closely siblings relate to each other—and how much more than rivalry characterizes the effects they have on each other's lives.

Siblings help each other in many ways. They often serve as role models for each other, teaching each other about social situations, what the rules are for sports, and how to deal with certain teachers at school, and frequently they offer each other the closest friendships that they'll ever know in childhood. Certainly competition and rivalry are also present. However, not all competition is bad or unhealthy: It can also lead to self-improvement and striving to be better at something than one is. Older brothers and sisters teach younger brothers and sisters how to do things, from riding bikes and dribbling basketballs to dealing with Mom and Dad when they're in bad moods.

It is certainly true that the arrival of a younger sibling dethrones the older sibling. Indeed, don't be surprised if, when a younger brother or sister is born, the older child regresses—sometimes using baby talk, wetting him- or herself, becoming more clingy, and in other ways acting like a baby. The older child must come to grips with the fact that there are other children in the world and that parental love has to be shared: not a happy idea at first, but one that marks an important step in the child's development. This is especially helpful for children entering the preschool and elementary school years, when they must adjust to many children. Older children may at first feel threatened by a younger brother or sister, but in the end siblings enable children to participate more fully and healthily in the social world.

While sometimes rivalry and competition between or among siblings can be corrosive and destructive, this is almost always because of the family climate, not because of anything inherent in being a brother or sister. People become angry and antagonistic toward and jealous of each other when there is a scarcity of supplies. In the case of siblings, those supplies don't have to be material; there can be a scarcity of love, safety, security, and attention from parents. Parental neglect and self-absorption, and an overall abusive and deprived environment, create a context in which siblings may quite viciously grab for what little they can get from the family's limited resources. Rivalry is also intensified when one child is favored over another, when unfair comparisons are made between siblings, or when the child's anger at the parents is displaced onto a brother or sister.

WHAT TO DO

1. Respect the uniqueness of each child in your family; realize that he or she is an individual with strong and weak points. Try to avoid comparing siblings to one another.

2. Allow a firstborn child to be your helper when a new baby is brought into the house. Help the older child to see that he or she can be a good role model and care-

taker. Share with the older child certain decisions that you make about the care of the younger sibling; for example, getting his or her input about setting up the baby's room, choice of toys, and even the baby's name.

3. Try to spend time alone with each child, or if this is impossible, make sure that you regularly focus full attention on each child separately, even if it's only for a few minutes at a time.

4. If siblings have conflicts, allow them to resolve them on their own. This is good practice for dealing with the rest of the world, and it also keeps you out of the fray.

5. Be sure that your experience of being an older or younger or middle sibling doesn't color your responses to your own children prejudicially. For example, if you are the second-born, you may naturally be more sympathetic to your younger children and feel less empathy for your oldest child's experience of being dethroned. Be aware of this so that you don't unwittingly favor one child over another.

6. Remember that destructive sibling rivalry is almost never natural, but rather the children's response to deprivation in their environment. If you see intense and bitter rivalry between your children over an extended period of time, you need to look at yourself, your child-rearing techniques, and your relationship with your spouse to get a better understanding of causes. You may well have to make some fundamental changes in your home life; these are never easy, but often they are the best—or even only—answer to improving your children's emotional lives and their connections to you and each other.

SEE ALSO

FIGHTING

CHAPTER FORTY-THREE

Adoption

"I hate you! I'm gonna run away from here and find my real mommy and daddy!"

There probably isn't a parent in the world whose children haven't at one time or another shouted, "I hate you, Mommy and Daddy!" But when the child is adopted (and knows that he or she is adopted), this angry outburst can be particularly devastating. Adoption is much more common and open than ever before, and most adopted children adjust very well to their homes and adoptive parents. However, adopted children do with some frequency evince emotional problems and difficulties that are carried into adulthood, and these appear to stem from some common feelings: that they weren't loved enough by their biological parents to be kept by them and/or that they aren't loved enough by their adoptive parents now (fearing they might be rejected or "given back"). These difficulties intensify with adoptive parents who haven't sufficiently explored their own motives and conflicts about adopting children—conflicts that their adopted children sense and respond to.

We do know that the earlier a child is adopted, the less likely it is that the child will experience emotional problems—problems that usually take the form of behavioral disorders. This doesn't mean that a child adopted at any age can't make a successful transition or adjustment, but it does suggest that certain issues need to be addressed with a child who is adopted at an older age. Some difficulties may arise from the fact that these days adoptive and biological parents more frequently know something about each other, and adopted children who want to find out about and meet their biological parents are now more able to do so, a result of freer access to records. In addition, a far wider variety of adoptive parents exists than ever before, including single, gay, and lesbian parents. All of these have impacts—sometimes positive, sometimes negative—on the adopted child and his or her family.

Every adopted child who knows he or she is adopted has similar questions: "Where do I come from? Why was I given up? Who are my real parents? Did I do something bad to be given up, or is there something inherently bad in me that made my real parents want to get rid of me? How much do my adoptive parents really want me now? Do they love me as much as a real parent would? Will they reject and abandon me the way I was before? How safe am I?"

These questions quickly make it clear that certain insecurities and self-esteem problems are common in adopted children—especially the tendency to feel "bad," unlovable, or defective. It is common for adoptive children to live a double mental life, both concerned with their outward lives with their adoptive families and involved in a secret fantasy life about who they imagine their "real" parents to be. Sometimes birth parents are exalted into royalty or movie stars or are idealized in other ways, especially in comparison with their actual adoptive families and home life. This inner life is often also one in which their feelings of being rejected and abandoned are heightened; they know the "real truth" about themselves, which is that they weren't good enough to keep and only just acceptable enough to adopt. These unresolved questions and conflicts can lead to real problems in their outward home life. They may feel great anger at adoptive parents, which is not truly anger at them, but rather anger at their biological parents for having abandoned them. They may threaten to find their biological parents and idealize the life they would then have with their "real" parents. (This is similar to the anger the child of divorced parents frequently feels toward the custodial parent, and the idealized image the child often has about the absent parent. The present parent becomes a kind of scapegoat for anger that has much wider roots and aims.)

Adoptive parents often have conflicts they need to address as well. They may not have resolved all of the issues that brought them to adopt in the first place. Some adoptive parents may continue to resent the fact that they could not biologically give birth—a resentment they may unwittingly pass on to the adoptive child. They may be angry at themselves or their spouses for their infertility. There may be issues of stigmatization or legal problems that interfere with an optimal attachment to the adoptive child. Some adoptive parents don't feel they deserve a child because they were unable to conceive one. Their unresolved grief about this may induce them to see the adopted child as foreign and possibly intrusive; this may increase when the adopted child is a different race or comes from a different ethnicity, culture, or nationality than their own. These conflicts are usually not conscious—indeed, most adoptive parents rationally believe they have done a good thing by adopting a child—but their inner conflicts can take a toll on the child they've taken into their life and home.

Thus it's important to realize that emotional problems the adoptive child may face are often inextricably tied to emotional problems adoptive parents have brought to the mix. Add to this the adoptive parents' anxiety that biological parents may one day have influence over the child, if only genetically (e.g., worrying that any aggressive behavior is something inherited from the biological parents), and it's not surprising that so many children feel there is something "wrong" with or "bad" in them. Some adoptive parents have lifelong worries about the intrusion in their adopted children of characteristics inherited from the biological parents— which again can't help but alienate the adopted child.

WHAT TO DO

1. It is crucial that you examine any unresolved issues you may have about not having your own biological child. Have you resolved your grief? Do you compare your adopted child to your fantasized biological one? Do you feel "deficient" and undeserving of having a child? Are you worried that your child may have inherited "bad" genes even though you rationally know this is foolish? You need to be honest with yourself about your own motives and assumptions to be sure that you're not unwittingly passing on destructive messages to your child.

2. Remember that the odds are that your adopted child will grow up to be just fine and, indeed, much happier and healthier than he or she would have been had the adoption not taken place. The odds are that you have helped the child greatly by taking him or her into your home.

3. Be as open as possible with your child about the adoption. It is now considered common sense that the child be told as early as possible—but not too early for the child to understand. Be relaxed and calm as you explain why you adopted the child and what you know about the child's biological parents. You might congratulate the biological parents for having the sense to provide your child with the happy home and prospects you can now give the child—that this was an expression of love for the child, not of rejection.

4. Be prepared for your child's questions to change as he or she grows older, and be prepared for the possibility that your child may want to seek out his/her biological parents. Do not react critically or anxiously; field your child's questions with calmness, love, and genuine concern for his/her feelings. Understand that your

child is simply seeking a fuller sense of his or her own identity. Also be prepared for the possibility that the biological parents may try to contact the child—a much more common phenomenon and one, again, that need not threaten you or your child.

CHAPTER FORTY-FOUR

Stepfamilies

"Don't tell me what to do—you're not my mother!"

The little girl who screamed this at her new stepmother re-inforced one of that woman's most nagging fears: that de-spite having married a man she dearly loves and to whose family life she very much wants to contribute in the most positive ways possible, she will not be able to have any nor-mal maternal relationship with that man's children. That woman is not alone in her worries; neither is her stepdaugh-ter in her anger. Given the rate of divorce (the outcome of 50 percent of American marriages), it is perhaps not surpris-ing to hear that 12 percent of all American children live in stepfamilies. These new families represent complex psycho-logical units that bring many different emotions to the sur-face among all concerned parties: the remarried couple, the children of each of the remarried partners, and the children's noncustodial parents. Although *The Brady Bunch* might be what some people wish were the model for these reconsti-tuted clans, it doesn't begin to suggest the complications and difficulties stepfamilies face in real life.

It is sometimes difficult for the two adults who have looked forward to the remarriage with such eager anticipa-tion, optimism, and love to understand that their positive feelings are not by any means shared by all the other people in their lives, specifically their children. Children tend to feel competitive with a parent's new spouse, who is often seen as a rival for affection rather than as a potential family member who might love them and whom they might love in return. From toddlers to adults, children whose parents have divorced tend to harbor the (usually quite secret and unspoken) hope that their parents will someday reunite. A remarriage puts an unwelcome halt to this fantasy, however positive the child may try to feel about it—or even rationally understand is appropriate to feel about it.

Interestingly, some view the stepparent's relationship to stepchildren as a species of adoption; indeed, it is called "intrafamilial adoption" (a term that also means adoption by grandparents, uncles, aunts, etc.) in certain psychiatric quarters. This suggests the stepparent needs to be sensitive to the child's anger and despair at not being with a "real" parent, as well as go to considerable lengths to make that child feel loved and respected.

Of course, the stepchild has many worries that are different from those of the adopted child (who typically has no relationship with his or her biological parents). For example, the stepchild may feel that liking the new stepparent means that s/he is being disloyal to the noncustodial parent. Children brought from one household into another who must also deal with stepsiblings often feel competitive with each other, each regarding the other as interlopers. In addition, there is frequently conflict between stepparents and noncustodial parents over the treatment of each other's biological children.

While these conflicts may at first appear to be insurmountable, in fact stepfamilies offer quite rewarding opportunities to forge new bonds and new ways to cooperate within the unit—all useful lessons to take out into the world. Since these new families are proliferating, we might do well to put energy into welcoming the challenges they represent rather than bemoaning their difficulties.

WHAT TO DO

1. Remember that it will probably take some time before both marital partners and stepchildren adjust to each other. Attempting to coerce intimacy or closeness is counterproductive, as it will only increase hostility and anxiety. Allow the new family to sort itself out; patience is the watchword.

2. If you're a divorced parent who is dating someone new and believe it may lead to marriage, let your children know about this possibility before introducing them to your newfound companion.

3. Allow your children to express their feelings to you about this new person, positive and negative. This will help your children to see that you're there for them, no matter how angry or ambivalent or unhappy their feelings may be.

4. Remember that the older a child is, the harder it will probably be for him or her to grow accustomed to a reconstituted family. Younger children seem to be more malleable and flexible in this regard.

5. Stepparents should realize that possibly a long period of "testing" will ensue after the new household has been set up. No one conversation with either stepchildren or one's own biological children will lead to complete conflict resolution; it will take many such conversations over time to do so. Stepparents should be in communication with noncustodial parents to make sure that they don't appear to be embattled or in opposing camps. In general, all channels of communication should be kept as open as possible, even if what gets expressed through these channels is often angry or hostile. Be patient.

6. Do not expect to be accepted as an authority figure right off in the new household. This position must be earned over time, and it is paramount that you both respect your stepchildren without undue expectations and attend to the needs of your biological children. If your stepchildren are a particularly difficult discipline problem, bring the issue up with your partner, and have him or her address it directly with his or her children.

7. Understand that some stepchildren may never adjust to the new family. You need to respect their points of view and not attempt to force them to feel or think differently.

SEE ALSO

DIVORCE

CHAPTER FORTY-FIVE

Children of
Depressed Parents

*"Uh, Mom? Is there anything to eat? Why? I'm hungry,
Mom. What? Oh. I'm sorry. No, it's all right. I know I
shouldn't be so selfish when you don't feel good. I said I'm
sorry, Mom. I—I'll find something in the refrigerator. No,
don't get out of bed. It's all right. I know you don't feel
good. I'm sorry, really . . ."*

Melissa isn't some spoiled child asking for yet another
between-meals snack—she is hoping for dinner. But she
knows from past experience—which has lasted most of
her nine years of life—that when her mother is in one of her
"moods," there's no talking to her. At those times Melissa
pretty much has to look after herself. She manages. She's
even getting used to it. What choice does she have? But the
moods are lasting so long these days. It seems like her mother
never gets out of them anymore. The worst part is that
Melissa feels it's all somehow her fault. That, like her mother
says, if she just weren't so selfish, if she just weren't always
thinking of herself, her mother would be happier, life would
be normal—maybe she'd even feel she could invite one of
her friends over. (Maybe she'd *have* a friend to invite over.)

The child of a depressed parent is in a terrible quandary.
It's bad enough for nine-year-old Melissa. But imagine being
five, four, two, or one. Imagine being an infant in the arms
of a mother who communicates no warmth, no love, no
affection—no emotion more passionate or engaged than irritability. As you grow, you adapt because you must—and a
part of that adaptation may be to tread lightly so that you

don't do anything to worsen your parent's dark moods. Slowly you even become convinced that those moods are your fault. You don't exactly know what you're doing wrong, but since nothing helps and everything you do just seems to make things worse, what else can you conclude except that you're to blame?

Not all children of depressed parents walk on eggshells, of course. It is well known from research studies (mostly centering on children of depressed mothers) that such children have a higher likelihood of developing a whole range of psychiatric problems, from depression (especially depressive episodes by the time of adolescence) and various forms of introversion to behavior disorders and hyperactivity. Like Melissa, these children frequently have low self-esteem and often feel criticized and blamed not only for their parent's condition, but for anything that goes wrong in the house. Many of these children also have decreased intellectual abilities due to delays in cognitive development caused by the parent's lack of involvement, encouragement, and interest. They tend to have a lower tolerance for frustration in general and suffer from more medical and physical complaints—as well as accidents—than children without a depressed parent.

Once again, the more severe and chronic the depression, and the younger the child when it begins, the worse it is for the child. However, when depression is combined (as it usually is) with hostility, family conflict, and poor communication with other family members, the outcome for children is even bleaker. In their depressed states, parents are so absorbed with their own symptoms—their worries, hopelessness, and overall sense of doom—that they withdraw and become unavailable to the child. They are rarely attuned to their child's burgeoning developmental thrusts and feelings. A child's healthy development depends crucially on healthy and loving verbal and physical interaction with parents or caretakers, but with the depressed parent, such interaction is usually minimal and sometimes absent. Depressed parents are unable to set limits for older children or otherwise structure their day. Their self-hate and self-loathing are displaced onto their children, and they appear to hate or to blame the children when in fact they're hating the negative feelings—projected onto their children—that they really have about themselves. In other words, the anger of a depressed parent, despite its apparent external target, is often really a species of self-hate. But that's far too sophisticated a concept for a little child, who knows only that Mommy is screaming at *her*. The child registers this hate as proof of her own unacceptability, intensifying her shame and guilt. The nightmare often worsens: Depressed people tend to marry depressed spouses, and the resultant marital discord can be truly horrific, often exploding into anger and violence. It is no wonder that so many children of these marriages tend to suffer the various pathologies that they do.

WHAT TO DO

1. If you are aware that you or your spouse is depressed, you must get professional help as quickly as possible. The good news is that great strides have been made in the treatment of depression, with a variety of antidepressants now available that, in concert with psychotherapy, have led to widespread improvement in formerly depressed people. However, you have to take the first step, and if you have children, it is urgent that you do. Psychiatric research has proven conclusively that children of depressed parents are at the highest risk of suffering long-term psychological pathology. Do it for your child.

2. Even if you are depressed and haven't sought help for yourself, strive to be aware of any symptoms in your child of the various psychiatric problems mentioned above—early signs of low self-esteem, negative self-

image, behavioral abnormalities, hyperactivity—and seek help for your child. Do the same if your spouse is the one who is depressed and hasn't yet gotten assistance.

3. If you know that your depression is interfering with your ability to interact with your child—especially around important developmental milestones—then make sure that others are there for the child during these important times. Enlist the aid of friends and other family members to give your child the needed attention.

4. You can to some degree lessen the impact of your depression on your child by going through the motions—adhering to normal schedules, making the bed, keeping appointments, and so on. Giving in to the depression, withdrawing to your bed, and shutting down will both intensify your own depression and have a devastating impact on your child. If your episodes of depression are manageable enough, strive to keep home life normal.

5. Your child's anger, hostility, and/or violence—even if you are not sure that it relates to depression—is a sign to change your behavior and restore calm to the home. Your children are more harmed by these episodes of hostility and anger than you may know. Once again, if you can't do it for yourself, do it for them.

SEE ALSO

DEPRESSION AND MANIA   BEHAVIOR DISORDERS

CHAPTER FORTY-SIX
Children of Alcoholics

*"How come you never invite me over to your house, Billy?
You're always coming over to mine. What's the problem—
your mom a witch or something?"*

Billy's mom isn't a witch, although Billy privately feels she often acts like one. But he won't invite his friends to come over not only because he never knows how his mother is going to act—if she'll be passed out on the couch or stomping around in a rage—but because the house is always such a mess, with empty glasses, bottles, and dirty dishes everywhere. He usually tries to clean it up himself, but it's a losing battle.

A losing battle indeed. In recent years, a great deal of attention has been paid to children of alcoholics, and it seems clear that the legacy an alcoholic parent passes on to a child can be cripplingly damaging in two ways: the physical effects of alcohol on the fetus when the mother drinks, and the emotional effects of living with an alcoholic parent, which generally take a terrible toll on his or her children. The physical effects have been empirically proven more than the emotional ones, but the emotional ones are undeniable.

Some studies indicate that as many as 20 percent of adults lived with an alcoholic parent growing up, and an additional 25 percent have been exposed to alcoholism either through another family member or via some other close personal relationship. About 13 to 15 percent of adults in our country can be labeled problem drinkers (if not alcoholics). With such percentages, it is not surprising that there are fully twenty-five million children of alcoholics (COAs) in the

United States. At least seven million of those are children under eighteen years old.

We know that COAs show up at psychiatric clinics and even medical hospitals more often than peers who have not been exposed to alcoholism. COAs suffer more injuries and poisonings and use outpatient medical services at higher rates than non-COAs. Being the child of an alcoholic increases the possibility of suffering from any of the following syndromes—attention deficit disorder, learning disorders, other behavioral disorders, depression, and anxiety in one form or another. These children are also at higher risk of becoming alcoholic or addicted to other substances themselves. They are more likely to have somatic problems, such as headaches and stomachaches. There is a greater likelihood that COAs will be sexually, physically, and/or otherwise abused or neglected by their parents, as well as encountering problems in cognitive, language, and speech skills, difficulties in expressing themselves emotionally, impaired school performance, trouble sleeping, and inability to reason or use good judgment; there is even a higher-than-usual incidence of epilepsy in COAs. These unfortunate children are more likely to feel helpless, perplexed, dependent, isolated, and "different"—unable to cope with many of the day-to-day challenges and requirements that other children manage to navigate with little or no problem.

Children of alcoholics often feel that they have somehow caused the problems that actually result from the parent's alcoholism. Confused about expectations—which change mercurially, depending on the parent's state of inebriation—these children experience a high degree of inconsistency and insecurity in their home lives. Like Billy, they are embarrassed and ashamed about the problem at home and often can't talk about or share their secret with anyone else. Consequently they often have fewer friends, and in what friendships they maintain, they tend to be either withdrawn or aggressive, to defend or lash out (two main modes of response they have learned at home). Clearly, having an alcoholic parent can take a terrible toll on the child's development. However, it is important to remember that not all children of alcoholics suffer from the aforementioned difficulties, illnesses, and impairments. Indeed, it is a wonder that so many COAs show the resilience that they do.

Alcoholic parents do a pretty poor job of parenting, starting with biology: The most dramatic effect of the impact of alcohol on the fetus is the development of fetal alcohol syndrome (FAS) during the pregnancy of a mother who drinks heavily. Such children have some degree of developmental delay in cognitive skills, if not overt mental retardation. They are smaller than other children and often have abnormal nervous systems and facial features. They don't sleep well, suffer from seizures, don't learn as well, have attention problems, and don't speak as well. Nor are they able to cope as well with daily problems as other children. Heart, neurological, immunological, and bone problems as well as hernias and urinary and genital abnormalities are all more common in children with FAS.

As has already been implied by the huge range of difficulties listed above that COAs tend to face, there are many other issues that affect the overall parenting abilities of the alcoholic parent. Alcohol induces violence in families; abnormal mood swings, financial strains, constant fighting, social isolation, poverty, and physical illness all plague the family with an alcoholic parent or parents. Those who abuse alcohol tend to abuse other substances as well, and suffer from what are known as co-morbid psychiatric illnesses. In other words, alcoholics have a higher rate of other mental illnesses, especially depression and anxiety. As stated, their children also have a higher rate of becoming alcoholic, an apparent intergenerational transmission that has led to much recent research about whether alcoholism is genetically inherited (although it is still difficult to determine what is the result of environmental conditioning and what is the result of biology).

WHAT TO DO

1. Clearly, if you are an alcoholic parent, your most immediate task is the obvious one: You must do whatever it takes to stop drinking. Avail yourself of the many options open to you, ranging from support groups such as Alcoholics Anonymous (which has one of the highest rates of helping people maintain abstinence from alcohol) to psychotherapy. Psychotherapy is also important for the other psychiatric problems you are more likely to be facing as well. You need outside help—probably in specific parenting skills as well as with kicking your habit—and the sooner you pursue that help, the better it will be for your child.

2. Your child also needs help. Al-Anon and Alateen (support groups based on the same principles as Alcoholics Anonymous) have proven to be enormously helpful to children of alcoholics in helping them to see that the problems plaguing both children and parents stem from a disease over which neither parent nor child has any control. Your child may also need psychiatric evaluation and possibly psychological tests; it is likely that he or she suffers from a range of problems such as those covered in the foregoing overview, and will need attention appropriate to whatever the specific problem(s) may be (emotional, school, social, developmental, etc.), including individual psychotherapy, support and group therapy, occupational therapy, remediation, special education, and possibly family therapy.

3. If you are not a parent but a concerned observer, you might discuss your concerns with the child's teacher, a clergy member, or another authority that you know the child's family respects—perhaps he or she can investigate what artful intervention might be possible.

This is always a difficult task; the well-known phenomenon of denial in alcoholics often tends to make the parent resistant to such intervention, but some alcoholic parents are already at such a low point emotionally that they welcome outside help. Clearly, if the child appears to be suffering from acute abuse, such intervention not only is advisable but may be essential. If possible, seek the counsel of an authority familiar with the disease of alcoholism who also has some direct connection with the family in question.

4. It is important to support any alcoholism prevention strategies in your community, schools, and religious institutions. If none are in place, taking measures to see that they are instituted and employed will be of incalculable benefit. One of the greatest weapons against alcoholism and its effects on children is education—and disseminating the clear message that help and support is publicly and privately available.

SEE ALSO

CHAPTER FORTY-SEVEN

Children of Parents
Who Are Physically Ill

"Every time I try to bring the subject up with Mikey, he just shuts down and says he doesn't want to talk about it. I know he's terribly upset. When I go to the hospital for treatments, my husband says he has nightmares, or he can't sleep at all. My husband has tried to talk with him about it, too—but, well, if we just mention the word cancer, Mikey's out the door."

When it comes to illness, the most familiar and even soothing family scenario has to do with a loving, healthy parent taking care of an ailing child. However, when that scenario reverses, especially if a parent becomes seriously or chronically ill, the effects can be devastating for both parent and child. The assumption or hope that Mommy and Daddy will always be there receives a body blow. If the child happens to be going through a developmentally appropriate period of separation anxiety when a parent gets sick, the effect on the child can be almost intolerably painful.

Indeed, the age of the child determines to a great degree how s/he can be expected to respond. The younger a child is, the more likely s/he will be to believe that s/he might somehow have caused the parent's illness. A young child may also be hyperconcerned about his or her own health or the health of the rest of the family. (The child's thought is that if Mommy and Daddy can get sick, then *anyone* can.) Older children may be able to seek out and tolerate hearing more information about the illness and appear on the surface to be able to handle it, but we shouldn't underestimate what's going on inside: The emotional impact can still be assumed to be devastating, even if the child is able to repress or hide it. Other children, like Mikey, may not be able to tolerate even the mention of the parent's illness, or may in other ways attempt to deny its existence.

The child's underlying personality is equally important in determining how ably s/he will be able to handle the impact of a parent's serious illness. Predictably, the child with a strong and resilient sense of self will react better than a child prone to intense fear and anxiety or who in other ways suffers from preexisting problems. Children with preexisting psychiatric difficulties will probably exhibit a flare-up of symptoms. Children with developmental problems—especially cognitive ones—will have more trouble understanding what is going on and probably will suffer acute anxiety. Gender also appears to affect the child's response: A girl tends to react more traumatically to her mother's illness, a boy to his father's. Naturally, another important factor in determining the response of the child is the nature of the parent's illness, the degree and kind of impairment the parent suffers from it, and of course the effects of whatever treatments the parent must undergo, particularly if they remove the parent from the home for long periods of time and/or if they lead to disfigurement (surgery, treatments for cancer, etc.).

Finally, the child's response is crucially affected by how the family unit—especially the parental couple—handles the illness. A spouse's reaction to the illness as well as the reaction of the sick parent him- or herself have a predictably huge impact, particularly when preoccupation with the illness leads to withdrawal from the child. While some parents are able to be fairly stoic, to contain or control their emotional distress, others may become acutely distressed and upset—which predictably intensifies the emotional trauma for the child. Parents need to remember that, especially for very young children, they are the bedrock of a child's life; there is no greater blow to a child's most fundamental sense of security than the threat of a parent's serious illness. As difficult as it may be to carry out, great care should be taken with how the child is told about the illness and how parents deport themselves and deal with the impact of the illness in front of the child.

Some children who learn of a parent's illness develop stress responses due to high levels of anxiety: sleep disturbances, intrusion of frightening or upsetting thoughts, and/or severe avoidance or withdrawal. Other children develop depression, anxiety, and even somatic symptoms that mimic the symptoms of the ill parent. Loss of appetite, angry outbursts, increased fighting, social withdrawal, and academic problems all constitute common reactions of a child to the trauma of a parent's illness.

WHAT TO DO

1. The most important thing a parent can do is to explain as clearly and simply as possible the nature of the illness and what the child might expect regarding it, including possible time spent away from the home in the hospital, any physical ramifications (hair loss from treatment for cancer, etc.), and possible changes in the parent's availability or household routine. It's equally important to emphasize what the parent will still be able to do (play with the child, help with homework, etc.) as well as reassure him or her about home life routines that won't change—meals (Saturday night will still be pizza night) and meal times, playtime, weekend activities, and so on. Also emphasize whatever the optimistic prognosis for the illness will be.

2. Whatever you tell children about your illness and however you attempt to reassure them and anticipate their most likely anxieties, your children will still have

reactions, some of which may include quite distorted understandings and expectations of what will happen to you. Encourage all family members to vent these anxieties, and correct any distortions so that each of you has a realistic picture of the illness and how it will affect you and everyone in the family.

3. Whatever family or household routines can be continued should be continued. The traumatic impact of a parent's illness on the child will be mitigated by doing as much as you can to keep home life as consistent and normal as possible. However, if certain routines must be changed or stopped, or if the parent's illness will cause some degree of financial stress, with the result that the family will not be able to afford certain activities, this should also be calmly discussed and made to seem like the family challenge it is. Enlist your children as allies; listen to their suggestions about how you may be able to save money or come up with less expensive alternatives to routines you may no longer be able to afford. Emphasize the positive even here.

4. Consider getting help to keep other aspects of home life going that you may no longer be able to do— employing someone to help with cooking and cleaning, or engaging someone in the neighborhood who may be able to drive a child to Little League, dance class, or swimming lessons.

5. Prepare your child for any potentially disturbing changes that may happen to you, especially physical ones, and reassure your child that these changes are simply part of the progress of your illness and/or the process of its treatment. If you must be in the hospital, make sure your child visits you; explain, or have your spouse explain, that being in the hospital means getting care that is not possible elsewhere. Emphasize its positive rather than negative aspects.

6. If your spouse is present, s/he has a great responsibility to act as a balance between you and your children—to communicate with them when you may not be able to do so, to reassure them, to keep family life as consistent as possible, and so on. This will not be easy for either you or your spouse, but the care taken with children about the effects of the trauma they are experiencing ultimately will have a salutary effect on you as well. Helping them to be calm and optimistic will very likely help you to be too.

7. Make sure that you and/or your spouse keep an eye out for any signs in your child of serious psychiatric, social, or academic problems. To this end, it may be a good idea to let the school know about the illness, so that they also can be on the lookout for problems that may need treatment.

SEE ALSO

STRESS   PSYCHOSOMATIC DISORDERS
DEPRESSION AND MANIA   ANGER
ANXIETY   FIGHTING

CHAPTER FORTY-EIGHT

Children of Gay Parents

"Hey, Mom? My teacher says we gotta write about the different stuff we learned from our mother and father. Um— any ideas?"

Janice's mom is a lesbian; Janice's other "mom" is her mother's life companion—another woman. Her family life is about as happy and complicated and full of ups and downs as any other child's life, but her mother's homosexuality does have an impact on Janice's life that children with heterosexual parents don't encounter. While there has been a dramatic upsurge in the number of children who are raised by gay parents—accurate statistics are impossible, but it is estimated that 15 million children have gay or lesbian parents (as many as 6 million lesbian mothers and 3.5 million gay fathers)— the assumption that one's parents are straight is still pretty well entrenched. Janice's fourth-grade teacher doesn't assume that all of her students come from intact nuclear families (plenty of her kids come from divorced or single-parent households), but in giving this homework assignment, she does assume that each child has and knows something about a mother and a father. Janice is the product of artificial insemination, and the only parents she has ever known are two moms.

Changing assumptions is something with which every family that includes a gay parent has an intimate acquaintance. And, with the proliferation of gay parenting, there are a lot of usually fearful and very deeply rooted assumptions to face and attempt to change. One of the greatest general worries is that gay parents automatically raise gay children (note the implicit homophobia—few people worry that heterosexual parents will automatically raise heterosexual kids). In the case of this belief, a misapprehension is wed to the fearful idea that it is "unhealthy" for a child to have a gay parent. Sometimes this is a veiled reference to the assumption that a gay parent will sexually abuse a same-sex child. This is very nearly opposite the reality: Sexual abuse of children is far more common with heterosexual than with homosexual parents. Indeed, there is nothing to suggest that gay parents automatically have any negative impact on their children. Children of gay parents develop normal gender identities, the usual range of (as in the general society, predominantly heterosexual) sex roles, bond well, get along with other children well, and in general do not have higher rates of psychiatric or behavioral disorders than do children of heterosexual parents.

It's not that there aren't problems. Indeed, because many gay parents are single parents (see the chapter on single parents for an assessment of some of the challenges here) and because no gay parent escapes having to deal with some societal stigmatization (for example, awkwardness at PTA meetings and parent-child events), undeniably there are various day-to-day hurdles particular to the gay parent–child household, one or more of which each such family deals with. However, no negative effects of gay parents on their children have been found automatically to occur. Quite the contrary: The greater tolerance for diversity, wider perspectives, and empathetic and often ingenious problem-solving abilities gay parents pass on to their children are clear assets, not liabilities.

It is unsurprising that the greatest problem that children with gay parents face is the persistent stigma they receive from others in the community. They are prone to be teased and made fun of by fearful and ignorant peers, and sometimes other parents. This is particularly difficult for children who—especially in the latency phase (roughly ages five to eleven)—desperately don't want to be thought of as different. Children may resent the fact that they don't have a "normal" family, that they're not like other kids—a common dilemma in the gay parent–child relationship. The stigma may be particularly acute because of a general ignorance in the community. Encountering a gay-parent household often provides the first one-on-one exposure to this sexuality that heterosexual families have. Most "out" gay people live in urban environments; the many gay parents with school-age children who live in smaller towns and villages and participate in social and school activities where being "straight" is taken for granted are often regarded as alien interlopers. One hopes that this prejudice will abate as more and more people in the general population realize how loving, nurturing, and normal so many gay-parent families are.

WHAT TO DO

1. If you are a gay parent, helping your child to accept your sexuality obviously depends upon your own self-acceptance and examination of motives to be a parent. It is strongly advised that you consult the chapter on single parenting for a fuller discussion of this. Such issues as dating—which for gay parents often requires going to a nearby larger city and participating in the gay bar culture (antithetical, in many people's minds, to a family lifestyle)—need to be addressed directly, and examined for their impact on both parent and child. Luckily, especially in urban areas, there are many social and support groups for gay parents (similar to the heterosexual Parents Without Partners groups) that offer various welcome alternatives.

2. It is almost impossible to grow up gay in this society and not experience some form of homophobia, which is just as typically internalized and turned into a species of self-hate. As with the single parent, the gay parent must address any unresolved issues about

his or her sexuality and motive for having children—
therapeutically, if necessary—so that unexamined insecurities and fears are not unwittingly passed on to
the child.

3. The age at which you should tell your child about the
   homosexual aspects of your relationships should be
   developmentally appropriate. Just as a heterosexual
   parent is ill advised to give sexually explicit details to a
   child too young to understand or register them, the
   gay parent should guard against any similar inclination
   to tell all before the child is able to assimilate the information. This does not mean staying in the closet
   about being gay. Indeed, it's strongly advisable to make
   the general fact of your orientation seem an easy and
   normal phenomenon to your child. Just be careful
   about pressing on your child more-intimate details in
   some anxious but misguided mission of total honesty.

4. Keep in mind that the younger a child is, the more
   accepting he or she will be of your homosexuality. It
   becomes increasingly difficult to break the news to a
   teenager at a time when he or she is undergoing
   struggles about his or her own sexuality.

5. Empathize with the difficulties your child may be
   having being accepted at school, clubs, and other
   social venues. You may want to take measures to edu-
   cate other parents and community organizations, perhaps most effectively by participating in them and
   demonstrating your authenticity as a parent, person,
   and contributor to the community. Helping out at a
   school bake sale or car wash can often do more to
   combat hostile feelings and fear than standing on a
   street corner waving a sign about the injustice of homophobia. The more you bond with various people
   and organizations in your community, the easier it
   will be for you and your child.

6. "Where do I come from?" questions from children of gay parents often present special challenges, particularly now that artificial insemination is so much more common than it used to be, especially for gay parents. Issues about the sperm donor's identity (if it is not known) can ape the issues an adopted child faces, although we don't yet have any statistics to indicate any definitive similarity in terms of emotional problems or distress. However, as a child matures and wonders about his or her origins, such questions will have to be addressed. The creative gay parent who has established a loving bond with the child and a freely expressive atmosphere will almost always be able to wing whatever question the child brings. (Consult the chapter on adoption for a fuller discussion of this.)

7. There is a burgeoning number of books and other literature written for gay parents, and some inventive children's books aimed at the kids of gay parents, that should prove to be helpful. These can be found in any large bookstore and especially in gay/lesbian sections.

SEE ALSO

ADOPTION   SINGLE PARENTS

CHAPTER FORTY-NINE

Child Physical Abuse

"No, Mrs. Martin, it's nothing, really! I just fell off the front step of my house and bumped my head. Please don't call my mom and dad. . . ."

Jimmy is hoping that his fifth-grade teacher won't call his parents to inquire about the bruises all over his face for a very sad reason: He knows that this would probably just lead to more bruises. Jimmy is the victim of child abuse—a frightening, humiliating, and shameful experience for him, and one he's always trying to cover up. He never invites friends home because he can't predict how violent his father will be; at school he comes up with excuse after excuse for why he's so often black and blue.

Parents who abuse their children physically typically have very little tolerance for frustration. They flare up easily; they have little control over their anger. They might hit a child with their hands or a belt, a strap, an electrical cord, a paddle, or whatever other weapon is at hand. They may burn the child with cigarettes, hot irons, or scalding water. Some abuse leads to serious injury and even death. Despite the fact that all states have stringent laws against child abuse, most parental child abusers commit the abuse over very long periods of time and are repeat offenders. The effects on the child are usually devastating: In addition to anxiety and depression, the abused child is usually also prone to violence, lacks trust in human relationships, and is impaired in language, speech, and IQ.

Abusive parents were almost always abused as children by

their own parents. They typically believe they deserved the abuse, and pass their own feelings of low self-esteem and guilt on to their children—not only reinforcing the cycle of abuse (making it more likely that their own children will grow up to be child abusers) but intensifying feelings of shame and self-hate in both parent and child. The relationship between parent and child becomes more complex because the parent, still caught in his or her own early childhood conflicts, often seeks help resolving those conflicts from his or her child, seeking to have the child fulfill needs never met by the parent's own parents. When the child goes along his or her own developmental way, the abusive parent registers this as a shock—the child is not "paying attention" to the parent, and the parent lashes out in anger and hurt. The child's own guilt increases, as s/he senses s/he is not giving something crucially important to the parent without ever having a clear idea of what that something is.

Another cornerstone is a stressful environment. This stress may be triggered by substance abuse, being a single parent (although it is not known precisely why, child abuse is more common among single parents), money problems, and so on.

Risk factors also proceed from the parent's unmanageable anger and feelings of resentment or hatred. To assess their own possible potential for abusing a child, parents need to consider the following questions: Have you become increasingly violent lately? Are you prone to throwing tantrums, and are they coming more quickly? Do you not get over your anger as you used to? Have you developed a particular grudge or hatred toward a particular child? Are you beginning to fantasize violence against that child? Are you feeling more isolated from a particular child, turning your back on him or her because of your fear that you may lash out violently if you do not? Any parent who answers yes to these questions needs to seek help immediately.

WHAT TO DO

1. If you're a parent who displays any of the warning signs just mentioned, and if your life is particularly stressful, and if there is a particular child whom you are finding more annoying than usual, it is essential that you speak with your doctor, go to a hospital emergency room, call a psychiatric or mental health professional, or ask for referrals from a trusted friend—and do it now. If you're alone and feel you have no one to call, call your local child abuse hotline. This is not easy because of the feelings of shame and fear that no doubt assail you, but it would be far worse to jeopardize the health and well-being of your child.

2. If you use spanking as a form of punishing your child, stop it immediately. Spanking gives only one message to children: that when a child has a particular need or desire with which you don't agree, it deserves a violent response. Not only does this cut off communication with your child, but it teaches the child that a violent response is an appropriate response to the expression of need, which it never is. Spanking can also escalate into something out of control, especially if substance abuse is involved. It may be hard to stop this form of punishment, but it is essential that you do. If you can't, seek immediate help.

3. If you see that a child is being abused, you must take measures to have the abuse stopped. This is usually a very difficult, awkward, and delicate task, because it will involve accusing a parent of the abuse, thus subjecting yourself to counterattack. However, the intervention could be life-saving for the abused child, and it is crucial that it be made.

4. Be equally careful not to abuse your child verbally—
   which also can have devastating consequences. Destructive criticism, humiliation, and screaming at the
   child all constitute emotional abuse, which can set
   the stage for a whole lifetime of psychological problems, pain, and distress. Although your feelings of
   anger and vindictiveness may be aimed at the child,
   you need to see what is causing them in yourself—
   which will probably require seeking individual
   psychotherapy.

SEE ALSO

DEPRESSION AND MANIA   BEHAVIOR DISORDERS
ANXIETY   ANGER
SEXUAL ABUSE   SINGLE PARENTS

CHAPTER FIFTY

Discipline

"I just don't understand, Doctor. Frankie would never act this way around us—he knows we'd wallop him if he ever tried that stuff around the house. But this is the fifth time his teacher has called me to say he's disrupted the class by making noise and telling jokes. How many more times must we punish him before he behaves?"

Parents not only make the best diagnosticians and helpers for their children but also are their most important teachers. However, the lessons that stick with our children aren't always the lessons we think we are teaching them. Let's say a mother has had it up to here with her six-year-old son, who will not stop pushing his three-year-old sister off her tricycle. Mom has tried everything: telling him calmly to stop, threatening him with no television that afternoon, exiling him to his room, yelling at him—and still, every chance he gets, whenever his sister tries to play with her favorite toy, he's back there pushing her off it. Finally she loses it: "Come here, young man!" She picks him up angrily, throws him across her knee, and raises her hand to strike the first blow.

I can only hope that something will keep her from landing it, because what she's in the process of teaching her son has nothing to do with respecting the rights of others, treating a sister more kindly, or behaving well in general. What she is telling him is this: (1) when you get really angry at someone, you hit them; (2) when you really want someone to do something, you hit them. In other words, she's teaching her son that violence is an acceptable means of getting your way.

The goal of discipline is to guide, not to punish. In concert with the example you set through your own behavior (the parent's other, perhaps even more powerful way of providing a lesson), discipline engenders and cultivates a sense of morals in your children. In fact, how and for what reason children are disciplined constitute the most crucial factor in how children end up living and comporting themselves in the world: their ethics, how they treat others, how they behave at school and later on in jobs, how they will treat their own families.

No subject consumes parents more than discipline. I receive more questions about how much and what kind of discipline should be administered to children than about any other single topic. Parents worry about being too permissive and being too strict. They have heard good arguments for both sides. Too often they confuse discipline (the methods we employ to teach and guide our children) with punishment (those actions we take when rules are broken). Punishment is only a small part of discipline. Punishment is, however, much easier to mete out than thoughtful discipline—which may be one of the reasons parents resort to it when they do.

Discipline is the art of instilling in our children a set of values that teach them the limits of what is appropriate and inappropriate behavior, both at home and out in the world. It teaches that other people have feelings and that there are dangers in the world that must be dealt with in safe ways. A well-disciplined child can control his or her impulses, cooperate with others, be patient, and navigate his/her way in the world with a feeling of both external and internal control. A well-disciplined child retains his or her uniqueness (the aim of discipline is *not* to adhere blindly to the status quo) but has learned appropriate modes of behavior within which he or she can react and respond in his or her own personal way.

Parents need to remember that there are rarely absolutely right or absolutely wrong ways to behave in every instance and that the goal of discipline is more to cultivate a sense of responsibility and consideration (so that children can begin to make their own thoughtful decisions about how to behave) than to pass down from on high some immutable list of commandments. Discipline also needs to be age-appropriate. Expectations of a child's behavior and capacity for understanding right and wrong have to fit the child at his or her particular age as well as take into account his or her particular strengths and weaknesses.

The following are general categories of advice about discipline that can be applied to all children and parents—no matter what the particular discipline challenge they may face.

WHAT TO DO

1. Reward appropriate behaviors whenever you see them. Always support constructive aspects of your child's behavior. This may be the most important disciplinary tactic.

2. See discipline as a continual two-way street of teaching and learning, negotiating and respectful interaction. Do not see it as a "Do what I tell you!" communication.

3. Always explain expectations in a developmentally appropriate fashion. Be clear and concise. Don't use too many words. "That doll belongs to Ann—give it back to her" communicates to a five-year-old the intended message far more effectively than lengthy lectures on the evils of stealing.

4. Make it clear to your child that the aim of any disciplinary measures is to achieve or improve cooperation between you—not to instill blind compliance with rules (for example, not "Do it this way because it's right" but rather "Do it this way and you'll make life easier for the whole family"). Your goal is not to create an automaton.

5. Be receptive to your children's feelings about the discipline you employ. Understand that their anger and frustration are not only a form of resistance to doing something they don't want to do, but also a way to communicate to you what they want—and are part of a human relationship that for the most part should be gratifying.

6. Remember that rules are needed for safety as well as supplying a necessary feeling of control for the child. They cut down on chaos and provide structure. However, be flexible and open to negotiation even from the very start (from toddlerhood on). Offer alternatives when you can (e.g., "You can put your teddy bear away now or in fifteen minutes") that give your child a sense of engagement, choice, and cooperation in the discipline process.

7. Be a role model for your child. This is your most effective teaching tool. A child will always pay more attention to what you do than to what you say.

8. Let your child have a say in what the family rules and responsibilities ought to be. This is an enormous ego boost for children, making them feel useful, more powerful, and more empathetic toward both rule givers and rule breakers.

9. Remember how you felt when you were humiliated as a child because of some cruel act of discipline (few of us don't have a number of examples to draw on) before you decide on how to discipline your child. Speak compassionately, don't attack your child's character, and if possible make sure that the disciplinary action is carried out in private—not in front of other children or family members.

10. If you decide punishment is called for, always be sure that whatever rules the child violated had been stated

clearly and simply, always give a reason for why the punishment is being given, and don't impose punishment that isn't warranted by the infraction (e.g., six months without television, no allowance for a year, and similar punishments are generally excessive, and you probably won't end up enforcing them, which means the child won't believe you when you state them). Be consistent and unwavering but not rigid. Remember that punishment teaches only that a rule has been broken. Punishment should generally entail the withdrawal of a privilege, treat, or other enjoyable activity. See that it is employed immediately and is clearly linked to an explanation of the rule violation for which it is being imposed. Make it clear why the rule is important; the consequences of breaking it should make sense to the child.

11. Never use corporal punishment. It teaches that violence is acceptable. It tends to make children more aggressive. It can be physically as well as emotionally dangerous, particularly when parents lose their tempers. It actually decreases the remorse that other disciplinary measures might induce your child to feel. Do not hit because your father or mother hit you. Even when you are at your angriest and can only think about what your own parents would have done, do not hit your child. (If what your parents would have done was spank you, they were wrong.) If your anger is out of control, leave the room. If possible, make sure that another parent or family member who is more controlled deals with the child at that moment. Never verbally abuse a child; this, like physical force, has no place in discipline.

12. Remember that humor may have its place in discussing or even administering discipline, but sarcasm is just another form of hostility and verbal abuse.

13. Don't let guilt manipulate you (neither yours nor any your child may try to induce you to feel). Be as clear with yourself as you are with your child why the discipline is called for and what the positive results are that it is designed to achieve.

14. Don't give in to tantrums. This only teaches the child that they are an effective way of getting what he or she wants.

15. Time-out offers a useful breathing space, particularly with younger children (up to age five), since it helps to decompress tense situations quite quickly.

16. Incentives (ways of encouraging good behavior over the long term) are always preferable to bribes (treats given to get the child to do what you want in the short term).

17. Never lose empathy for the strong feelings of your children, even if they are expressed in ways that may upset you. Discipline is empty without compassion.

SEE ALSO

CHILD PHYSICAL ABUSE

CHAPTER FIFTY-ONE

Media and Children

"I'll be there in just a minute, Mom—it's almost over. No, I didn't say that a half hour ago! C'mon, Mom—just a little while more . . ."

Children spend an average of four to seven hours a day in front of the television. From the time it first became widely available in the 1950s, people have been concerned about the impact of so much television, worrying about everything from the passive audience it makes of our children to the effects of so much violence and sex—now rampant not only in movies and television dramas but in daytime TV talk shows. With the Internet now reaching millions more people— many of them kids—a whole new arena is consuming our children's interest and attention and time. As much as parents may attempt to limit their children's access to the more lurid excesses of TV and the Internet, blocking certain X-rated pay-per-view cable channels on TV or employing software to keep their kids out of adult chat rooms—children can be amazingly ingenious when it comes to getting around these blocks. A parent's credit card used on the Internet, Web sites that the child can access despite blocks that a parent may have attempted to impose, a friend (with less vigilant parents) who still has access to pornographic movies on television, and/or simply finding ways to watch network television nonstop for hours when parents are at work or away for an evening—generally, if children are determined, they will find ways to get around many of the media restrictions set by their parents.

What are the real dangers of all this exposure to the me-

dia? Studies have been inconclusive, but common sense—
and our own experience of seeing the deadening effect of so
much television on our own kids—tells us that the impact of
so much exposure to the media is far from positive. It is not
only the violence (80 percent of television programs have
been found to have violent themes) and sex on TV and the
Internet we have cause to worry about, but also the simplistic, flat stereotypes that so many talk shows make of complicated issues and the general way that the media don't invite
any rigorous thought or active engagement from our kids.
While studies have not determined whether aggressive children are made more aggressive by watching violence on television or whether aggressive children simply seek out violence
on television, TV violence undoubtedly is an exacerbating
influence on aggression and needs to be limited. The in-
escapable fact is that our television and computer screens are
not the baby-sitters we would wish for our children—much
as that's the function, by default, they've too often assumed.

The impact of the information age is so pervasive that it's
hard to determine all of its effects. The news media now
bring to our children graphic and immediate detail about local, national, and international disasters—bombings, shoot-
ings, natural disasters, war, murder, sex crimes, kidnappings,
suicides, and all the other stuff of nightmares. Basically our
society has become one in which a tidal wave of information
is flooding every one of its media outlets, with our children
providing one of its largest audiences. Even the most vigilant, well-meaning parents can't monitor their children's access to every new suggestive music video, television talk
show on child rape, or Web site on kinky sex that crops up.
But we can institute some attitudes and preventive measures
that, at the very least, may encourage our children to widen
their minds and come up with ways to entertain themselves
using their own inventiveness and curiosity—ways that don't
entail making a beeline for the TV or the computer.

WHAT TO DO

1. Parents need to take an active part in learning about the how and what of media to which their children are exposed. This means knowing what your child is watching on television and learning about computers and the Internet—an expertise your child may have far more of than you do. The first task for any parent is to see exactly what the media holds for your child so that you can then make some determination about what to limit in your child's exposure.

2. Start early in helping your child to develop healthy media habits. Set up rules in your house for limited exposure to television and to nonacademic or non-school-related Internet surfing. An average of one hour on the Internet and one hour watching television is reasonable.

3. Don't allow your television or computer to become a baby-sitter.

4. Be present when your child is watching television or surfing the Internet; be ready to enrich and deepen your child's understanding of the often simplistic information s/he may be getting from either source.

5. Work with your child's school in developing appropriate messages about the media and how to understand them, particularly about the dangers of Internet surfing and possible Internet-mediated seductions, never giving names or numbers to strangers on the Internet, and other related matters.

6. Dinnertime and after-dinner activities are all important occasions to bond with your kids. Don't have the TV blaring in the background, and don't let your child isolate him- or herself in a room with a computer or television after dinner. Devise activities, games, and discussions that engage all of you and keep you

busy with each other, not busy in isolation in a screen.

7. Cut down on the amount of television you wa possibly on the number of televisions you have in your house. As always, the model of behavior you set is your most effective teaching tool.

CHAPTER FIFTY-TWO
Single Parents

"Mom? Wait—don't leave for work yet! I can't find any socks. They're still in the hamper? You mean you didn't wash anything? That's four days in a row, Mom! You gonna work late tonight again? It's okay—I can let myself in. Dinner's the blue package in the freezer? Okay. No, I don't need a baby-sitter! I'm ten years old already! I can take care of myself."

There are more single-parent households now than ever before. Society has provided new avenues to make single parenting possible: More unmarried men and women, including gay men and lesbians, now adopt children. The high rate of divorce means that many families turn into single-parent households. More women have decided to have children outside of marriage, sometimes through artificial insemination. And of course single-parent families are created when one spouse dies.

Over the past few decades, the media—especially movies, television dramas, and sitcoms—have reflected this growing phenomenon, regularly featuring single-parent-family themes and stories (e.g., *Alice Doesn't Live Here Anymore, One Day at a Time,* etc.). However, they often give a skewed and romanticized picture of the very real difficulties a single parent and child(ren) typically face. If you are a single parent, nobody has to tell you that daily life rarely resembles a sitcom. The "Where's my socks?" vignette at the start of this chapter offers a far milder example of these struggles than it might have. Financial strains tend to be worse in the single-parent home, and poverty, with its many negative consequences for both parent and children, is a frequent affliction. Stress seems to be endemic: Studies have shown that single parents typically have higher levels of cortisol (a stress hormone) than parents who are partnered. Single parents tend to have more mood disorders, specifically depression, than other parents. Depending on how single parenthood is achieved—whether it's chosen or results from death or divorce—single parents often feel guilt, remorse, vengefulness, or otherwise hostile emotional states that not only intensify whatever mood disorders they may already have, but also tend to have a devastating impact on children. Child abuse tends to be higher in single-parent households than dual-parent ones. Children of single parents tend to have a higher incidence of behavioral and psychological problems than children of dual-parent households.

Indeed, the problems that children of single parents face cover a complicated and wide realm. There tends to be a higher incidence of depression, anxiety, feelings of loneliness, aggressive or violent acting out, psychosomatic symptoms, and academic failure in these children—all of which tend to be somewhat more prevalent in boys, who seem to adapt to the situation less easily than girls. However, as bleak a picture of single parenting as this presents, it's by no means the whole canvas. Many single-parent households are healthy, loving, and nurturing environments for children. In particular, single mothers who must balance work, parenting, and other responsibilities often feel invigorated, self-confident, and independent and demonstrate a rare resiliency and strength of character—all of which has an enormously positive impact on their children. As with every other parenting challenge, the many difficulties in single parenting can be seen as—and with ingenuity sometimes turned into—significant opportunities for growth for both parent and child.

WHAT TO DO

1. The most important task for the single parent is to seek help. Realize that you cannot take care of all your household and parenting responsibilities alone, and seek out friends, family members, and relatives— or, if you can afford it, employees—who can lessen the burden. Your children's prospects and happiness will be impaired if you ignore your own well-being.

2. As in divorce, if you've become a single parent after having been with a partner or spouse, it is important to help your children keep as much as possible to the same routines they followed before so that some feeling of familiar, normal family life continues. A sense of structured family life contributes enormously to the child's happiness and security.

3. Allow your child, if s/he is old enough, to offer a helping hand at home. Do not try overly to shelter your child from responsibilities that you may feel guilty s/he is taking on. Sharing chores and household tasks with your child makes you stronger allies and increases an important sense of bonding between you. A child who contributes to the welfare of the home also has stronger self-esteem—a feeling that s/he is needed—which will pay dividends in the child's life outside the home as well.

4. Similarly, as your child matures, don't shelter him or her from various stresses (financial, family, etc.) that you are dealing with from day to day. This does not mean overwhelming the child with inappropriate confidences or information s/he is not equipped to handle, but it does encourage you to give your child the sense of being a partner in the business of leading your shared lives.

5. Don't be afraid to discipline your child because you have a vague notion that a child who lacks the second

parent should be given a special dispensation or let off the hook. Appropriate discipline is important because it contributes to a sense of strong family ethics and structure, which your child needs and deserves. If you are a single parent, take measures to have a family member of the other gender visit regularly; perhaps this person can help you discipline your children on occasion if you feel you need help.

6. Avail yourself of the wide range of literature and support groups addressed to single parents. There are also many such support groups for children, a listing of which can be obtained from your local mental health association.

7. Because of the increased tendency in children of single parents to develop certain psychiatric disorders (covered above), be on the lookout for symptoms— for example, of anxiety, depression, social isolation, and academic failure—and get help for your child from your school or mental health care professional.

SEE ALSO

DIVORCE	THE UNDERACHIEVER
STRESS	PSYCHOSOMATIC DISORDERS
DEPRESSION AND MANIA	BEHAVIOR DISORDERS
ANXIETY	CHILD PHYSICAL ABUSE

GLOBAL DISORDERS

CHAPTER FIFTY-THREE
Pervasive Developmental Disorder (Autism)

"I'm terrified, Doctor. Philip is almost two and he still hasn't said a word. Could he be . . . ?"

The good news for Philip's mother—who can't bring herself to ask whether or not her son might be autistic—is that, overwhelmingly, the odds are he is not. A severe disorder of childhood also known as pervasive developmental disorder, autism occurs somewhere in the range of two per ten thousand children. If a child is autistic, he or she will almost certainly present many symptoms besides the one (not talking) that worries Philip's mother—symptoms that nearly always appear far earlier. Probably because autism is one of a parent's most feared diagnoses, many parents and sometimes even pediatricians seem to deny, ignore, or rationalize these early symptoms. Unlike most babies, who from birth are social creatures—smiling, grasping, following Mommy and Daddy with their eyes, crying to denote distress and to get attention, entering in early childhood into complex social interactions with other children—autistic children do little or none of this. Autistic infants show far less interest in the human face. They often don't have the social smile that we otherwise see emerge in infants between one and two months of age. They seem to lack many of the attachment traits that other children are born with. As a result, from early on they appear to be less interested in human relations than other children, are very solitary, are unable to share, and seem not interested in connecting with anyone else. Associated with this is a very limited ability to communicate; verbal and nonverbal communicative abilities are impaired. Their capacity to express language or to receive (register, understand, respond to) it is severely curtailed. When they do speak, language is not used as a means of social interaction; it does not aid in their social development. Autistic children tend to speak in odd, highly personalized ways, with cadences and intonation that often strike the normal listener as bizarre. They frequently do not understand or respond to other people's speech.

Three-quarters of autistic children are also mentally retarded, with IQs ranging in the 30s, 40s, and low 50s, with little or no capacity for abstract thought. Interestingly, despite this overall deficiency, some autistic children have islets of unusual ability that differentiate them from the purely mentally retarded child. Known as savants, these children may have extraordinary aptitude for music or mathematical calculation, a seemingly infallible memory for dates and schedules, or similar abilities. However, these abilities are unconnected to any sense of context and, once again, do not improve or have much effect on social skills.

Behavioral problems associated with autistic children encompass a wide and complex variety. Most salient is the odd intensity of fixation on whatever single thought, possession, or activity absorbs them—a fixation that excludes all human interaction (e.g., an autistic savant with an encyclopedic knowledge of baseball statistics will often speak of and appear to think of nothing else). They often become attached to inanimate objects rather than people (blankets, balls, pieces of wood, etc.) and will not tolerate separation from whatever the object is. They are generally hypersensitive to sensory stimuli—sounds, food aromas, textured surfaces, and the like—preferring things that they can feel and taste over anything more abstract or purely visual. They often rock, walk on their toes, flap their hands, tend to mutilate themselves, and evince odd and idiosyncratic gestures. They don't relate to whole people or objects, rather tending to relate to parts of a person or thing. They are usually compulsive and inflexible, frequently preoccupied with turning lights on and off, going in and out of closets, and similar ritualized behaviors that can go on for many hours. They have an obsessive need for regularity and sameness; we often see panic in autistic children whose feeding or sleeping schedules are the least bit altered or who see that a piece of furniture has been moved. Many of these children are aggressive and prone to angry outbursts or temper tantrums. Their moods swing widely, and they tend to be hyperactive.

As with so many other psychiatric syndromes, we don't know the exact cause of autism, but we do know that it is not caused—as had once widely been thought—by cold, inattentive, negligent, or unloving parents (the "refrigerator mother" theory of autism, which held that most autistic children came from the upper socioeconomic strata, with parents who were presumably uninterested in nurturing their children). Children with autism come from all sorts of parents. It seems to be a disorder connected with dysfunction in the central nervous system. While no clear lesion or specific neurotransmitter has been isolated as the cause, we know that genetics plays a role. Occasionally illness seems to be implicated (such as encephalitis, phenylketonuria, tuberous sclerosis, fragile X syndrome, difficult births, and mothers who had rubella during pregnancy). About a quarter to a third of autistic children have elevated levels of serotonin. Many of these children have what are called soft neurological signs that come out during examination, such as problems with right-left coordination, laterality, attention span, and motor overflow.

WHAT TO DO

1. Treatment for autism should start as early as possible and will probably continue for a lifetime. Even in the best of cases, where there is improvement in language and social skills as the child reaches adolescence and adult-

hood, residual social, educational, and occupational difficulties persist and will always require attention.

2. A broad-based, multimodal psychoeducational intervention constitutes the treatment of choice. A therapeutic nursery school for preschoolers (allowing children to participate in a wide variety of interactions) and other educational, psychological, occupational, physical, and language therapies should be instituted early on. Various medications have been used, although no one in particular has proven curative or dramatically effective. There has been some success with the major antipsychotic medications, although results have not been consistently positive and effective. Many autistic symptoms can be dealt with behaviorally at the moment they arise.

3. If you think that your child might be displaying some early signs of autism, go to your pediatrician and also consult a child psychiatrist. They will ensure that your child receives a complete physical and psychiatric examination and evaluation. Be sure that your child gets a hearing test, neurological examination, language evaluation, and psychological tests. All concerned professionals will combine their expertise and tell you if in fact there is cause for concern.

SEE ALSO

SCHIZOPHRENIA

CHILDREN WHO DON'T SPEAK

LANGUAGE DISORDERS

INTELLIGENCE

ATTACHMENT DISORDERS

OBSESSIVE-COMPULSIVE
  DISORDER

ANXIETY

ANGER

DOES MY CHILD NEED TESTING?

ALL TYPES OF THERAPY

PSYCHOTROPIC MEDICATION
  AND CHILDREN

CHAPTER FIFTY-FOUR

Attachment Disorders

"I always have to tell Jennifer to stay with me when we go out to the store. She's always walking up to strangers and bothering them! I don't think she should talk to everyone she sees. I worry she'll get into big trouble one day."

Jennifer, eight years old, may simply have an outgoing temperament—but Jennifer's mother says her behavior isn't a sometimes thing. She's constantly pushing herself on people, demanding attention wherever she goes, and otherwise inappropriately barging in. It's possible she may be exhibiting what we call disinhibited attachment disorder—one of two attachment disorders (the other is inhibited attachment disorder) that afflict children.

It is common knowledge that a healthy attachment between a child and his or her parents forms the bedrock for the child's physical, emotional, and psychological development. Children are born with certain inborn traits that enable them to make this all-important attachment: for example, the ability to cry (which signals parents about their needs), smile, follow their parents with their eyes, and grasp with their hands. As the infant bonds through breast-feeding and being held, changed, and bathed, more and more complex forms of attachment evolve until the child has developed a strong and stable relationship with parents. This not only helps the child to feel cared for and protected, but enables the child to engage and form healthy relationships with other people.

There are many reasons that healthy attachments don't form or go awry at some point during a child's development. Separations from parents, hospitalization of children, a parent's physical or mental illness or problems with substance abuse, abusive parents, and sometimes simply a poor fit between the temperaments of parents and their children all can lead to inadequate feelings of attachment early in life. No attachment is ever 100 percent adequate—none of us has a perfect bond to our children or our parents—but most of us form relationships that are adequate and fulfilling. We learn to feel safe and loved enough to dare to go out into the world and form healthy relationships with others.

For some children who have not received good enough care—indeed, for whom care has been markedly inadequate—the result is an attachment disorder, defined as a disturbance in social relatedness that is a response to the disregard of a child's needs for comfort, stimulation, and affection. Sometimes even the physical needs of the child are disregarded, or there are so many separations from the primary caregivers that the child is unable to form any stable attachments in or out of the family.

Disinhibited attachment disorder (the form Jennifer may be exhibiting) is a disorder in which children form diffuse relationships, indiscriminately attempting to bond with whomever they come into contact with. Such children show no selectivity in their attachment pattern, often talking to anyone on the street and exposing themselves to danger by attaching themselves to possibly dangerous people.

The other form of this disorder—inhibited attachment disorder—manifests in a number of different ways. Children with this disorder tend to be confused, perplexed, fearful, and anxious, and yet may appear to be hypervigilant as well. They give conflicting responses to people in relationships and are always on guard, as if expecting something terrible to happen. They are not easy to comfort and sometimes show what is called "frozen watchfulness," in which they simply stare or exhibit other unusual abnormalities in their gazes.

Most children with an attachment disorder show an unusual form of relating to people before they are five years old. They often are exceptionally aggressive, are unable to control their feelings, cannot sustain attention, are easily distractible, and have a low tolerance for frustration—traits similar to those in children with attention deficit disorder. They also show a similarity to children with language disorder in that they often repeat words and have poor articulation. These children are sometimes confused with those who suffer from pervasive developmental disorder, but with the latter we don't see the grossly pathological care (traumatic separations, abuse, neglect, parental illness, etc.) that we always see in children with reactive attachment disorder. Because children with this disorder also tend to have IQs that are lower than normal, they are sometimes mistakenly confused with mentally retarded children.

This is one general realm of disorder in which it can be clearly stated that environment, not biology or genetics, is the cause. Children with attachment disorders typically come from homes in which there has been severe caretaker deprivation, maltreatment in the form of physical or sexual abuse, and/or physical and emotional neglect; these disorders also appear in children who were brought up in institutions. The good news about this is that when children are relocated to less pathological environments in which there is loving care, stimulation, and the presence of other positive factors that were lacking in the earlier environment, they will nearly always respond in a favorable way. In other words, these attachment disorders are treatable, even reversible, to a large degree. Indeed, one of the diagnostic criteria we use to differentiate reactive attachment disorder from other severe disorders is the speed with which many of these children correct their poor attachment behavior when they experience greater care and nurturing in a different, more beneficent environment.

WHAT TO DO

1. If you're reading this book, it is unlikely that your child suffers from an attachment disorder, which al-

most always occurs in households in which little or no care is shown for, or interest taken in, a child's welfare.

2. If you see signs of overly inhibited or disinhibited attachment behaviors, it's most important that you reflect on your child's temperamental type to be sure that this is in fact not just evidence of his or her natural personality. There are some children who are slow to warm up to other people and seem more fearful and anxious when they enter new situations; these children likely do not have reactive attachment disorder but are simply shy by nature. In addition, there are children who are aggressive, assertive, curious, a bit overly active, and a bit impulsive, but within normal limits.

3. Reactive attachment disorder is one of the most serious psychiatric disorders seen today. If you feel your child suffers from it, you need to consult a professional immediately. Parents who adopt abused or neglected children or who offer them foster homes may especially have to be on the lookout for this disorder. Offering a more loving environment will undoubtedly be helpful to the child, but he or she still will need professional help to overcome past damage from the earlier unloving environment.

4. Remember that children with inhibited and disinhibited attachment disorders were not born that way. This is one of those syndromes that is clearly related to the care the child receives (or does not receive).

SEE ALSO

INTELLIGENCE   SHYNESS
PERVASIVE DEVELOPMENTAL   SOCIAL PHOBIA
    DISORDER (AUTISM)   CHILD PHYSICAL ABUSE
ATTENTION DEFICIT DISORDER   SEXUAL ABUSE
LANGUAGE DISORDERS   THE PHYSICALLY ILL CHILD
BEHAVIOR DISORDERS   ARTICULATION DISORDER

CHAPTER FIFTY-FIVE
Schizophrenia

"I often lived in a fantasy world when I was a little boy—doesn't that just mean you've got a good imagination? But my son, Andy, can't seem to snap out of it. I can't follow what he says most of the time; sometimes he just makes nonsense sounds again and again. He says he keeps seeing these flying creatures. And he doesn't seem to know how to play with other kids—they say he's 'creepy.' His teacher said she was afraid he might be schizophrenic, but that can't be true, can it? He's only seven!"

Nearly all young children conceive elaborate fantasies that often have little connection to reality. They may have trouble thinking logically or in an organized way, shifting from topic to topic without warning or sense, holding on to beliefs that appear to us to be outrageously unfounded. For the most part, these "crazy" thoughts and behaviors are part of the child's perfectly normal grappling with various developmental stages—indeed, they are healthy evidence of an abundant and creative imagination. By seven or eight years old, most children think logically, and although they may hold on to various beliefs, superstitions, and fantasies that strike us as unreal, they are generally pretty well grounded in reality.

Unfortunately, some children are afflicted by persistent delusions and suffer impairments in thinking and perception that do not go away. Like Andy's father, parents see evidence of this in many areas—irrational or disorganized speech, poor social interaction, difficulties at school, inattention to personal hygiene. These children may suffer from a severe disorder, or psychosis, that indicates a fundamental impair-

ment in the child's ability to grasp reality. One of these disorders is called schizophrenia.

Schizophrenia usually has its onset in late adolescence or
early adulthood. Although it is rarely seen under the age of
five and almost as rarely seen in preadolescent children as a
whole, recently there has been an increasing number of psychiatric reports of children who appear to suffer from schizophrenia. Like adult schizophrenics, children with this disorder
have both auditory and visual hallucinations, although children are more likely to see bizarre things than to hear strange
voices in their heads. Children with schizophrenia often have
powerful irrational beliefs about their parents, may see monsters and ghosts, and may experience other visions and
sometimes voices that urge them to do harm to themselves
or engage in "naughty" behaviors that will bring on punishment. The child may become paranoid that the air or his/her
food is poisonous, or that other people or creatures are
watching and conspiring against him or her. These delusions
often induce heightened anxiety, agitation, panic, and sometimes violent or suicidal acts. The child will appear to be
highly disorganized—the product of a thinking disorder
meshed with frightening hallucinations—and it will be difficult to follow the child's speech or logic. Feelings and behavior will not appear to go together: The child may laugh at
inappropriate times, or otherwise evince dissociative emotional reactions that appear incomprehensible or seem to
have no provocation. Many schizophrenic children move or
grimace strangely, with odd mannerisms, unnerving facial
expressions, and ritualized gestures that make their presentation even more bizarre. There may also be what are called
"negative symptoms," which convey a flattened or con-
stricted spectrum of emotions; these children appear not to
enjoy anything, speak little, look blankly ahead of them, and
avoid any contact with others, to the point of complete social withdrawal.

We do not know what causes schizophrenia, although

various biological and genetic influences appear to be at least partially causative. Studies of the brains of schizophrenics— particularly of blood flow to the cortex region—have recently yielded some information about possible brain structure abnormalities, such as enlarged brain ventricles. Studies indicate there may be causative abnormalities in the neurotransmitters of schizophrenics as well. Until recently, most research on schizophrenia has focused on the psychodynamics of communication that occur in the family of the schizophrenic: inconsistencies, "double-bind" communications (mixed messages), and other anxiety-producing phenomena that may induce schizophrenia. Environmental factors have also been studied, including socioeconomic status and divorce or single parenthood.

We do know that schizophrenia is associated with developmental difficulties in children and often with learning, attentional, speech, and behavioral disorders and problems. Indeed, it can often look like other disorders, and the professional must differentiate this illness from other syndromes that mimic some of its signs and symptoms, such as mental retardation, depression, mania, and such afflictions as attention deficit, speech, language, pervasive developmental, behavioral, and sometimes even seizure and obsessive-compulsive disorders. (Chapters covering these topics should also be consulted.)

WHAT TO DO

1. Professional help is always needed. Over the years there have been many interventions that have helped, including treatment with psychotropic medications, special education, family therapy (whose focus is understanding the disorder and helping parents with their own anxiety about it), and individual and behavioral psychotherapy for children.

2. Be prepared for the fact that the schizophrenic child will require a multifaceted approach both at home and psychotherapeutically, and that you will need to participate in the child's treatment in a variety of ways.

SEE ALSO

GETTING HELP

CHAPTER FIFTY-SIX

All Types of Therapy

In our discussion of many of the topics and issues covered in this book, particularly about the more severe behavioral and psychiatric disorders that can afflict children, various types of therapy have sometimes either been suggested or (in the case of more serious disorders) indicated—with the suggestion to see this chapter for a rundown of what those therapies entail.

At first glance, those therapies cover a bewildering range not only of the illnesses they are designed to treat but of the philosophies and techniques they employ to treat them. In general, for a child who suffers from a specific learning disorder or speech impediment, help is relatively easy to find; through your doctor, your child's school, or your local hospital or medical clinic, you can easily find names of clinicians specifically trained to treat the disorder. However, when more general psychotherapy is indicated, even people who know the differences between a clinical psychologist, a child psychiatrist, and a social worker face a bewildering forest of conflicting opinions, credentials, possibilities, and prejudices. The fact seems to be that whatever the therapist's training, degrees, school of thought, or technique, the clearest indicator of successful treatment is how comfortable your child feels going to see him or her every Tuesday at 4:45 P.M. Because psychotherapy of whatever stripe depends upon helping the child feel secure, relaxed, and able to talk freely, the therapist-patient relationship is paramount. However, just the fact that the child gets along with someone is rarely enough (otherwise circus clowns would be doing a booming psychotherapeutic business on the side). It is obviously always wise to look for a therapist who has had specific train-

ing and experience in treating the emotional problems of
children. For children who require general psychotherapy
but also have ADD, learning, or behavioral disorders, the
therapist should have experience in those disorders as well.
Experts range from social workers and clinical psychologists
to psychiatric nurses and child psychiatrists. The most broadly
trained of these are child psychiatrists, but all of them—
depending on their experience and possibly further training—
can offer useful help.

It's probably as hard to find a good psychotherapist as it is
to find a good prospect for marriage—not an infelicitous
analogy, since both unions depend on strong, sustained intimacy and respect for their success. Certainly you should ask
your pediatrician and inquire at your school and local medical
institutions about recommendations. You should also consider personal recommendations from friends whose children
have received help that succeeded.

Sometimes just one visit can be clarifying—the therapist
may have so much knowledge of your child's problem that
direction can be given on the spot, and that may be all the
therapeutic advice you need. For longer-term therapy, you
should ask for and get at least a ballpark idea of how long the
therapist thinks the treatment will last, and make all the necessary inquiries about fees and insurance. Do pay attention to
your child's responses to the therapist as the sessions continue. If your child expresses an entrenched dislike of or discomfort with the therapist that lasts longer than several
weeks after the initial meeting, the strong likelihood is that
your child is going to the wrong person. Psychotherapy is a
subjective business, and feelings count.

Various forms of available therapy include:

1. *Individual psychodynamic therapy.* The most common
   type of treatment, this is the classic one-on-one
   therapy, with sessions that last from thirty to sixty
   minutes. Its focus is not only the amelioration of

symptoms, but a restoration of your child to his or her normal developmental track. Many different techniques are employed, often including play techniques, which will teach your child to identify feelings, master problems, face fears, and resolve conscious and unconscious conflicts. Parents play a crucial role; your bond with the therapist and your understanding of the therapeutic aims are important parts of what will help your child to get better.

2. *Family therapy.* Family therapy is based upon the idea that treating the child is effective only when the whole system of which the child is a part—the family—is also brought into treatment (an idea central to systems theory). Since so many of the emotional problems that afflict children are at least partly caused by family conflict and difficulties, family therapy has proven to be very effective.

3. *Group therapy.* Group therapies range from groups of people with a specific focus (children of alcoholics, abused children, shy children, skills groups, etc.) to psychotherapeutic groups whose aims are those of individual psychotherapy (amelioration of symptoms and return to the appropriate developmental track) but add the element of interacting with others, which can improve the child's social skills.

4. *Cognitive/behavioral therapy.* Cognitive/behavioral therapy concentrates on helping the child to see how s/he can change behavior and patterns of thinking to achieve new and more gratifying results. Treatment often involves exercises with specific aims. This is distinct from the psychoanalytic approach, which encourages a less directive focus. It is especially effective for children with behavioral disorders and ADD. Cognitive therapy has proven effective as well for mentally retarded children, bed-wetters, and children who are anxious or depressed.

5. *Hypnosis.* Hypnosis is not employed with children younger than school age; however, in older children it has proven effective in changing habits and helping children with obesity, headaches, and various stress-related syndromes.

6. *Biofeedback.* Biofeedback is a method used to help children regulate their bodily responses particularly with regard to muscles, blood pressure, and pain. It is an excellent adjunct for children who suffer chronic pain, including headaches.

7. *Special remediation.* Special remediation is required for children with learning disabilities, and should be administered only by professionals who have been trained in the appropriate technique. This is more than regular tutoring; it focuses on the specific information-processing difficulties found in children with learning disorders.

8. *Parent work.* Parent work is therapeutic work done with the parent either by the child's therapist or by another mental health care professional the child's therapist has recommended. It is employed when it is clear that both parent and child need therapy and that neither can improve unless both seek help.

9. *Hospitalization.* Children need to be treated outside the home in hospitals in the case of psychiatric emergencies, such as suicidal or homicidal behaviors, aggression that is out of control, psychotic disorders that are unmanageable at home, and sometimes pervasive developmental disorder. While in the hospital, the child will be evaluated by a team of professionals including psychiatrists, social workers, psychologists, and often a recreation and/or occupational therapist. The child usually receives a combination of therapies, including milieu therapy, crisis intervention, medication, and family, group, and individual treatment.

10. *Day and residential treatment.* Such treatment is often indicated for children with serious psychiatric problems that require supervision, either part time or full time, and a multimodal treatment including individual and group therapy and often medication and occupational therapy. Many of these children usually lack an adequate, safe, or healthy home environment, which residential treatment strives to provide them.

11. *Psychopharmacological therapy.* The use of psychotropic medication in children is covered in the next chapter.

CHAPTER FIFTY-SEVEN

Psychotropic Medication and Children

The use of psychotropic medications, which modify thinking, behavior, and mood, has been growing rapidly in our society due to a confluence of factors, including a shift in psychiatry to more of a biologically based attempt to understand people, a shift in the culture toward more rapid cures, and a shift in insurance companies' preference toward short-term therapies. All of these elements have made the treatment of targeted symptoms by medication a more popular mode of psychiatric intervention.

There is a raging debate about the safety of using psychotropic drugs in children, whose nervous systems are still maturing. There is also a dearth of long-term studies about the side effects of these drugs, especially in children. However, there is no question that these drugs help people, including young ones, each day in overcoming crippling symptoms. They help save lives, return people to work earlier, and help people adapt to their various roles in society occupationally, educationally, and socially.

Since psychotropic drugs are chemicals, you might think that we know the specific chemical abnormalities or so-called imbalances that lead to specific psychiatric symptoms. But there is no proven chemical imbalance yet that explains most of the common psychiatric symptoms that we see clinically. Additionally, we hear in university settings, at psychiatric conventions, and in the lay press that we know how psychotropic medications work. In fact, despite recent advances in our understanding of biological and molecular interactions, we still do not know specifically how and why particular medications help on that level. We hear much about receptor sites in the central nervous system, neurotransmitters (chemicals that circulate in and between neurons), and other phenomena, but we still have not been able to pinpoint the causes of most psychiatric illnesses or the specific mode of effect of most psychotropic medications. This should not necessarily dissuade us from accepting a psychiatrist's recommendation that medication can and will help, but it should temper our belief that our knowledge is any more advanced than it actually is. The brain is a difficult organ to study, and this fact retards research in the area.

There are quite a few different classes of medications that we call psychotropic, and drugs in a given class may be used to treat a variety of psychiatric syndromes. For example, an antidepressant marketed originally to treat depression may be used for people with anxiety as well. Additionally, confusion arises because a particular psychiatric syndrome may be treatable by different classes of medication. To make it even more confusing, often a person receives a combination of medications, and sometimes these combinations can include as many as three or four different psychotropic drugs. The most commonly used psychotropic drug classes are the following:

- Antianxiety medications (AA)
- Antidepressant medications (AD)
- Antipsychotic medications (AP)
- Mood stabilizers (MS)
- Stimulants (S)

The symbols in parentheses will be used in the discussion of each medication below.

Either after an initial psychiatric evaluation with a child psychiatrist or during therapy with a psychiatrist or a non-psychiatric mental health–care professional, the question of the use of psychotropic medication may come up. The following suggestions should be kept in mind:

1. Psychotropic medication should never be taken by your child as the only form of therapeutic intervention. It should be seen as an adjunct to another form of therapy that is being administered.

2. Before taking psychiatric medication, your child should receive medical clearance, which at a minimum should include a thorough pediatric medical examination, blood tests including a complete blood count and liver function tests, and an electrocardiogram. You must inform the doctor of any known medical conditions that your child has.

3. You should feel comfortable in asking the prescribing child psychiatrist about the following issues:

    a. The names, both brand and chemical (generic), of the medications being prescribed for your child.

    b. Whether in fact this medication has been approved for use in children. You should keep in mind that most psychotropic medications have not been formally approved for use in children, because most of the studies prior to marketing were done in adults. This does not preclude the use of such medication in children, but the child psychiatrist should be able to answer your questions about how many studies have been done, what the experience of clinicians has been regarding the use of this medication in children, and what his or her particular experience with this medication has been.

    c. What the dosage is and how it should be taken. Although most prescriptions will state dosage information on the label, you should feel free to ask more specific questions regarding use of the medication. For example, should it be taken on an empty stomach or after a meal? Is it safe to take with certain foods? What should you do if a dose is missed?

d. What the side effects are. You want to know what side effects are most common with a particular medication, remembering that most side effects are mild and transient. But have there been recorded long-term complications with the use of this medication? Are there acute and life-threatening side effects, and what are the signs of these? Most parents worry about whether a given medication is potentially addictive and what the signs of addictive or abusive use of the medication are.

e. What adverse interactions the particular drug might have with other medications that your child is taking or might be prescribed. Your psychiatrist should furnish you with a list of dangerous drug interaction potentials.

f. What the child psychiatrist expects from the use of medication. Also ask when the results are to be expected, when and how dosages will be increased or decreased, and what to expect with each increase or decrease. Specifically, you want to be sure to understand which specific symptoms are being targeted for relief so that you know how to judge the efficacy of a particular medication.

g. How much the drug will cost. You want to be sure that your psychiatrist prescribes for you the least expensive and most effective type of a specific medication. Generic compounds are generally cheaper than their brand-name counterparts, and insurance companies these days tend to favor generic drugs.

What follows is a listing of the drugs most commonly used for various specific psychiatric problems. Each class of psychiatric symptom or syndrome will be followed by the medications most commonly used. It should be noted that dosage regimens, common side effects, and the like will not be listed for a very specific reason: It is up to you and your child's psychiatrist to discuss the unique and individual mode of prescribing that will be done for your child. Each child, based on his or her medical history and presenting psychiatric symptoms, will deserve his or her own unique prescription profile. Dosages, potential side effects, drug interactions, and the like will be unique to your child, and will depend to some degree on the child psychiatrist's mode of prescribing. You will notice that many of the psychiatric problems for which prescriptions are commonly given require drugs from one or more categories. Do not be surprised if in fact your child receives such multiple prescriptions.

The following is a list of common psychiatric ailments and the most common, but not totally exhaustive, list of medications prescribed today in this country.

1. *Behavior disorders.* As you might remember from the chapter on behavior disorders, often aggressive behaviors emanate from a particular syndrome with which a child might be afflicted. Thus it's common that children who show aggression have a specific diagnosis, and this should be treated with the appropriate medication. In other words, if your child suffers from ADD, medication such as Ritalin (S) or Dexedrine (S) will be the treatment of choice. For other children the use of lithium (MS) and Tegretol (MS) might be prescribed. Drugs such as Thorazine (AP), Haldol (AP), or Risperdal (AP) might be tried, especially if your child has evidence of organic brain dysfunction and/or very severe impulsivity. Inderal, a medication called a beta blocker since it blocks neural excitability in the beta receptors of the autonomic nervous system, has also been used for aggressive behavior disorders.

2. *Insomnia.* If your child has one of the various forms of insomnia, your child's psychiatrist might prescribe

Dalmane (AA) or other medications from this group as well as Sinequan (AD) and/or trazodone (AD).

3. *Anxiety disorders.* These come in various forms, including panic disorder, which has been successfully treated with serotonin selective reuptake inhibitors (SSRIs) such as Prozac, Zoloft, Paxil, and Luvox (all ADs) as well as the benzodiazepines (AAs). In addition, BuSpar (AA) and Inderal (beta blocker) have been found to be effective.

4. *Phobias.* School phobia and various other phobias have responded well to Klonopin and Valium (both AAs). School phobia in particular has also been treated with Tofranil (AD) and Xanax (AA). Social phobia has been treated with Prozac (AD) and BuSpar (AA) as well as benzodiazepines (AA) and Zoloft (AD).

5. *Obsessive-compulsive disorder.* This illness is treated with various medications, often in combination. These include Prozac (AD), Zoloft (AD), Luvox (AD), Anafranil (AD), BuSpar (AA), antipsychotic medications, and trazodone (AD).

6. *Depression.* A host of different medications are used to treat children with depression these days, and often a combination of medications is employed. Most commonly children are treated with one of the SSRIs, specifically Prozac, Paxil, or Zoloft (all ADs), and sometimes with a drug from the class of medications known as tricyclic antidepressants, which includes Tofranil (AD). In addition, other medications such as Wellbutrin (AD) and Effexor (AD) have been used in children.

7. *Mania.* If your child also suffers from some degree of mania or hypomania along with depression, s/he has bipolar illness. Mood stabilizers are used both in the short term for children who are showing evidence of

manic or hypomanic symptoms or for long-term prevention of these symptoms. The most-used drugs include lithium, Depakote, and Tegretol (all MSs).
Additionally, sometimes antipsychotic medication,
which includes Thorazine, Mellaril, Haldol, Trilafon,
Risperdal, Prolixin, and Clozaril (all APs), is used.

8. *ADD.* If your child suffers from attention deficit disorder, the first line of drugs to be used would be Ritalin, Dexedrine, or Pemoline (all Ss). If these don't
work satisfactorily, your child psychiatrist will probably prescribe desipramine (AD), Wellbutrin (AD), or
clonidine (alpha blocking agent). Last, Prozac, nor-
triptyline, Effexor (all ADs), and BuSpar (AA) have
been tried.

9. *Schizophrenia.* If your child suffers from childhood
schizophrenia, one of the antipsychotic medications
will be prescribed. These include Thorazine, Zy-
prexa, Mellaril, Risperdal, Clozaril, Haldol, Prolixin,
or Trilafon (all APs).

10. *Pervasive developmental disorders.* Autistic children have
shown some benefit from the use of Haldol (AP),
fenfluramine (S), and even Luvox (AD) due to the
complexity of their syndrome and difficulty in treating it. They have also been tried on a host of other
medications, including the stimulant medications,
mood stabilizers, antidepressants, and other antipsychotic agents.

11. If your child suffers from Tourette's syndrome, the use
of Haldol (AP) is considered the first line of treatment; Orap (AP) is also used. Additionally, drugs such
as Klonopin (AA) have been tried.

12. For enuretic children, DDAVP (which affects pituitary hormones), often in the form of a nasal spray,
has been found effective, as has Tofranil (AD). Other

drugs such as desipramine (AD) have been tried with some degree of success.

13. Sleep terror disorder usually passes, but if its severity interferes with normal functioning at times, Valium (AA), Tofranil (AD), and Klonopin (AA) have been used.

Chapter Fifty-eight
Does My Child
Need Testing?

Various tests have been referred to generally in many of the chapters in this book, and this chapter will itemize the most common of them, explaining what they screen for and what conditions may make it advisable for the test to be administered to your child. Remember that these tests are not infallible and that intelligence tests, especially, often give only a partial picture of your child's intellectual potential (see Chapter 24).

Indeed, any test should be seen as an adjunct to a broader assessment of your child's development, abilities, and well-being. No test score should be seen as definitive. Much as a test of blood pressure gives only one aspect of a person's physical health, each single test makes sense only if seen in the larger context of other means of assessing the child. It is important that when you tell the child the results of these tests you emphasize what is positive about those results— possibly including the treatments or courses of action that the tests indicate will improve your child's functioning. These tests should not be made to appear as some sort of punishment, shame, or humiliation, or as if they have been administered because the child is "stupid." They should be explained as measures to help make decisions that will improve the child's life. Indeed, as diagnostic tools, particularly in the case of certain behavioral, psychiatric, and neurological disorders, these standardized tests have great usefulness; they will also help to indicate the most appropriate and effective treatments for your child.

INTELLIGENCE TESTS

Intelligence tests measure your child's ability to learn. The results are given as a numerical score (sometimes broken down into separate numbers for different types of intellectual abilities) that indicate your child's intelligence quotient, or IQ. The most common of these tests is the Wechsler Intelligence Scale for Children, known as the WISC, which measures IQ both as a single overall score and as separate verbal and performance scores; there are also subtests in the WISC that measure different mental functions. The Wechsler Preschool and Primary Scale of Intelligence, also known as the WPPSI, measures intelligence in younger children, ages three to seven. Also used is the McCarthy Scale of Children's Abilities.

ACHIEVEMENT TESTS

Achievement tests are sometimes given to determine if there is a disparity between a child's native intelligence and his or her performance in school (see chapters on learning disorders and on the underachiever) or to see if a child's achievement is appropriate to his or her age. To differentiate children with learning disabilities from those with low intelligence, these tests are often given in concert with intelligence tests, a combination usually referred to as a psychoeducational battery (i.e., if the child scores higher in intelligence than achievement, learning disabilities may be indicated). The most common ones are the Woodcock-Johnson Psychoeducational Battery, the Wide Range Achievement Test, the Kaufman Test of Educational Achievement, and the Wechsler Individual Achievement Test (WIAT). These tests for the most part measure achievement in reading, mathematics, and spelling.

ADAPTIVE BEHAVIOR

Adaptive behavior tests help to indicate a child's day-to-day living skills, ability to socialize with peers, and motor and communication skills. The Vineland Adaptive Behavioral Scale is one of the more common tests applied.

PROJECTIVE TESTS

Projective tests tap into various aspects of a child's psychological processes and give a good idea of any serious disturbances in mental functioning or deep psychological difficulties having to do with self-concept or relations with others. They are used predominantly as adjuncts to the clinical psychiatric evaluation and include the common inkblot or Rorschach Test and the Thematic Apperception Test (TAT).

ATTENTION DEFICIT DISORDER

Attention deficit disorder (see chapter on the topic) has become a focus of interest for testers due to the prevalence of its diagnosis. Certain tests are routinely used to help diagnose problems with attention and concentration, which are the major issues for children with ADD. These include the Continuous Performance Test, the Behavioral Assessment System for Children, the ADHD rating scale, the Home Situation and School Situation questionnaires, the child's Attention Profile, and the Test of Variable Attention.

SPEECH AND LANGUAGE ASSESSMENT

As chapters in this book covering the topic indicate, a child's speech and language abilities are often reliable indicators of overall intelligence. Speech and language skills are a crucial matter for development, and much time and effort is spent in the assessment of these functions. Common tests include the Peabody Picture Vocabulary Test, tests of language comprehension, the Developmental Sentence Score Test, the

Preschool Language Scale, and the Clark-Madison Test of Oral Language.

NEUROPSYCHOLOGICAL SCREENING TESTS

These tests measure perceptual motor problems, memory deficits, learning disabilities, cognitive deficits, and other incapacities that indicate the relationship between possible neurological deficits and a child's psychological functioning. They include the Bender Visual Motor Test, the Developmental Test of Visual Motor Integration, the Benton Visual Retention Test, and the Luria-Nebraska psychological battery test.

INFANCY AND PRESCHOOL DEVELOPMENT

The one test that measures the development of intelligence, motor functions, and behavior even in infants is the well-known Bayley Scales of Infant Development.

Remember that these tests should be administered by professionals who have a developed expertise. The interpretation of the results, the explanation to parents, and the recommendation of remedial measures when indicated are dependent on the testing professional's experience, sensitivity, and skills.

OTHER RESOURCES

Alcoholics Anonymous
P. O. Box 459
Grand Central Station
New York, NY 10163
212-870-3400

American Academy of Child and Adolescent Psychiatry
3615 Wisconsin Avenue, NW
Washington, DC 20016-3007
800-333-2676

American Speech-Language-Hearing Association
1801 Rockville Pike
Rockville, MD 20852
888-321-ASHA

Anxiety Disorders Association of America
600 Executive Boulevard, Suite 513
Rockville, MD 20852
301-231-9350

Autism Society of America
7910 Woodmont Avenue, Suite 650
Bethesda, MD 20814-3015
800-3-AUTISM

Children and Adults with Attention Deficit Disorder (C.H.A.D.D.)
499 Northwest 70th Avenue, Suite 109
Plantation, FL 33317
305-587-3700

Coalition for Quality Children's Media
112 West San Francisco Street, Suite 305A
Santa Fe, NM 87501
505-989-8076

Federation of Families for Children's Mental Health
1021 Prince Street
Alexandria, VA 22314-2971
703-684-7710

Learning Disabilities Association
4156 Library Road
Pittsburgh, PA 15234-1348

National Alliance for the Mentally Ill
200 North Glebe Road, Suite 1015
Arlington, VA 22203-3754
800-950-NAMI

National Alliance for Research on Schizophrenia and Depression
60 Cutter Mill Road
Great Neck, NY 11021
516-829-0091

National Association of Children of Alcoholics
11426 Rockville Pike, Suite 100
Rockville, MD 20852
888-554-COAS

National Center for Post-Traumatic Stress Disorder
215 North Main Street
White River Junction, VT 05009
802-296-5132

National Council on Adoption
1930 17th Street, NW
Washington, DC 20009
202-328-1200

National Depressive and Manic-Depressive Association
730 North Franklin Street, Suite 501
Chicago, IL 60610-3526
800-826-3632

National Enuresis Society
7777 Forest Lane, Suite C-737
Dallas, TX 75230-2518

National Institute of Mental Health
5600 Fishers Lane, Room 7C-02
Rockville, MD 20857
301-443-4536

National Mental Health Association
1021 Prince Street
Alexandria, VA 22314-2971

National Sleep Foundation
729 15th Street, 4th Floor
Washington, DC 20005
202-347-3471

Obsessive-Compulsive Foundation, Inc.
PO Box 70
Milford, CT 06460-0070
203-878-5669

Office of Health Communications and Public Liaison
National Institute on Deafness and Other Communication Disorders
National Institutes of Health
31 Center Drive, MSC 2320
Bethesda, MD 20892-2320
301-496-7243

Overeaters Anonymous
6075 Zenith Court NE
Rio Rancho, NM 87124
505-891-2664

Parents Without Partners, Inc.
401 North Michigan Avenue
Chicago, IL 60611-4267
323-644-6610

Selective Mutism Foundation, Inc.
PO Box 450632
Sunrise, FL 33345-0632
305-748-7714

Social Phobia/Social Anxiety Association
5025 North Central Avenue, Suite 421
Phoenix, AZ 85012

Stepfamily Association of America, Inc.
650 J Street, Suite 205
Lincoln, NE 68508
800-735-0329

Tourette Syndrome Association
42-40 Bell Boulevard
Bayside, NY 11361-2820
800-237-0717

HENRY A. PAUL, M.D., is a psychiatrist, educator, and author who has helped thousands of children and their parents for over twenty-five years. In addition to being in private practice, he is the executive director of the Karen Horney Clinic in New York City and the president of the American Institute for Psychoanalysis. He is on the faculties of the Mt. Sinai Medical Center and Columbia University, and he appears regularly on national television and radio programs. Dr. Paul is also a consultant to the New York City Administration for Children's Services and other child welfare organizations. He is the author of *When Kids Are Mad, Not Bad* and is the father of two children.